Real Estate on the **Brink**

MAKING MONEY IN DISTRESSED PROPERTIES

Skip Lombardo

PROBUS PUBLISHING COMPANY
Chicago, Illinois
Cambridge, England

To my wife and children—
the loves of my life.

Contents

Preface vii

Acknowledgments ix

1. Why You Should Invest in Distressed Real Estate 1

2. Selecting Your First Distressed Property 17

3. Sources of Hot Buys 41

4. Scratching Up Your First Down Payment 51

5. Nothing Down: Myths and Realities 71

6. How to Get the Loan You Need 85

7. The U.S. Government: Your Friend in Deed! 111

8. Nonjudicial Foreclosure 129

9. Buying Real Estate at Wholesale Prices 149

10. Auctions: Your Tool for Selling and Buying Properties 161

11. Condos and Co-ops as Investments 171

12. The Glorious Small Apartment Building 189

13. The Business of Real Estate Recordkeeping 211

Epilogue 221

About the Author 223

Index 225

Preface

Several years ago I read a book about real estate, and it changed my life.

I followed the advice of the author, who claimed that if I'd begin an investment program by buying a small, distressed apartment house, fix it up to increase its income, then trade it up to a larger distressed complex, I'd be on my way to a life of wealth and independence. All I had to do to finally arrive there, he prophesied, was to continue working the process until I reached the plateau of financial success I desired.

As it turned out, the author was right. With his book as my personal guide, my original $2,600 investment in a little triplex in North Hollywood, California, eventually mushroomed into millions of dollars of real estate.

Can this book do the same for you? I firmly believe it can—that's precisely why I wrote it. Opportunities in real estate are still abundant and real estate is still the most reliable source of wealth acquisition in our economic system.

The procedures described herein reflect the *current* real estate market. They're designed to guide you through a profitable investment program in the field of entry-level distressed property— houses, condos, co-ops, and apartments. All you need is self-confidence and the perseverance to work the same basic investment precepts I evolved after decades of trading in the field.

Although my methods are relatively simple and clear-cut, I identify some hazards and pitfalls you must learn to overcome, along with some personality traits you should try to cultivate to ensure your success.

All the "how-tos" you need are here: how to locate the properties; raise cash for a down payment; use special government programs to assist you—all those techniques and many more are contained within these pages.

I'm proud of the fact that my book is much different from others currently on the market. In my work, for instance, I suggest precise step-by-step procedures to follow in order to accomplish every operation discussed—how to deal with your lender in order to get the loan you need; how and when to buy a property in foreclosure; how to buy a property from a lender; how to make money in a multiphased project; how to thoroughly research a property; how to keep real estate records and for how long.

To ensure your success, I give you an inside track on the finer details of operating in real estate, everything from how to clean up your credit report to the construction of a no-down-payment purchase. My purpose is to enhance your self-image with knowledge so that you'll feel as though you're a veteran investor even as you go about your first transaction.

Our economy generates 100,000 millionaires every year! Down the road apiece, wouldn't you like to be one of them? Ongoing prosperity and financial independence are *not* reserved for the privileged few! In America those perks are available for everyone who cares enough to earn them. You've got to begin somewhere, and this book gives you a running start.

For professionals, semiprofessionals, tradespeople, businesspeople, homemakers—for everyone yearning to live the good life, to breathe the air of independence, to wean yourselves from a deadline or a boss—this book is for you.

You can start with next to nothing and build yourself an empire. It's possible. I did it. You can do it too—if you want it badly enough.

Acknowledgments

Special thanks to the staff at Probus Publishing for all their assistance in making this book a reality. I'd like to express my gratitude to Pamela Patchin Van Giessen for putting me on the right track, to Lynn J. Brown for keeping me focused, and to Jim McNeil for his encouragement and enthusiasm.

Why You Should Invest in Distressed Real Estate

To me, the terms *distressed real estate* and *golden opportunity* are synonymous. I can drive up almost any street, at any time, in any neighborhood, and spot potential money-making distressed properties ripe for investment. There's a never-ending supply of them out there. If you want to find out how to spot them, purchase them, and make money from them, read on.

When I use *distressed* to describe a certain property, I think of three key elements: condition, location, and environment.

Condition

The condition of distressed property is usually revealed by the extent of its deferred maintenance. *Deferred maintenance* means that the property, for whatever reason, is suffering from cosmetic and functional neglect. For example, it may need

- A good paint job
- A new roof
- The repair or replacement of major kitchen appliances
- Landscaping or tree removal
- The heating and cooling systems repaired
- New carpeting or flooring
- The refinishing of hardwood floors
- New plumbing or electrical fixtures
- Minor carpentry work
- New mirrors, window panes, shower doors, or tub enclosures
- Retiling of kitchen or bathroom counters
- A thorough cleaning

Timing is important in all the real estate transactions discussed in this book. For investment in distressed real estate to work well, you have to focus on accomplishing the rehabilitation (rehab) of property quickly. Whether you rent or sell the property, the time you spend completing the repair work will impact your profits.

Thus, I recommend that you select distressed properties whose repairs can be accomplished in no more than four weeks. As you gain experience with such repair jobs, you'll learn how to coordinate tasks and subcontractors so that more than one repair can be accomplished at the same time. If repairs will require longer than four weeks, consider whether the property is too far gone and unsuitable for investment.

Usually, presenting a property to a prospective renter or buyer before it's completely renovated is a waste of time. No matter how graphically you explain what repairs you're making, the current disrepair of the property is what sticks in the prospect's mind.

Deferred maintenance does *not* mean structural faults that resulted from an inept architect's plan or a poorly executed room addition. Unless you're an experienced building contractor who can accurately assess the costs of correcting major deficiencies, stay away from properties with such problems. Deferred maintenance also excludes improper or illegal "do-it-yourself" projects that previous homeowners undertook. (Most local governments have enacted building codes that define precisely how property alterations or additions should be made. Be sure previous owners observed these rules.)

If you become interested in a property that looks like it was altered, make sure you ask the owner whether the improvements were made with the proper permits and were checked by a building inspector who verified that the changes met code. You can also call the local government's building department and find out for yourself. If you learn improvements were made without proper permits and inspections, your offer to buy the property should require the current owner to obtain the permits, have an inspection, and bring the property up to code. Otherwise, a later buyer can require *you* to make the changes at your own expense.

Improving the property's exterior is another major endeavor, whether it be installing a sprinkler system, replacing tired landscaping, adding fencing, or resurfacing a driveway. If the distressed property includes an in-ground pool, deferred maintenance may require you to replace a heater or filter—but not the pool itself.

The careful, tasteful improvement of the exterior of a property can produce substantial net profits.

Location

When seasoned real estate professionals preach "Location, location, location," they aren't just spouting truisms. Today more than ever, location is the key to successful real estate investing.

In your quest for a distressed property, put yourself in the position of a future renter or purchaser, then ask yourself, "Would I rent this house in this neighborhood?" or "Would I buy it?"

If you can answer "Yes!" to both questions, odds are that, all other factors being favorable, you'd be wise to make the purchase.

Environment

Generally, never buy distressed property in an area whose environment is beyond your control. For instance, avoid property located in a crime-ridden or slum area, on heavily traveled roads, or within earshot of an expressway. Moreover, property located below flight patterns of aircraft from the nearest airport is excluded from the category of distressed property here.

Buy distressed property only in well-groomed, viable neighborhoods. Look for the ugly duckling surrounded by swans. Always ensure that your prospective project isn't adjacent to another distressed property. It's pointless to spend money to improve property that is surrounded by properties that will drag down its value.

In summary, distressed property is well-located housing in need of cosmetic and functional refurbishing.

Now that you have a good idea of what distressed property is and isn't, the following information should convince you to take control of your future and make the personal commitment to initiate your first investment.

Benefits of All Real Estate Investments

Long-term stability, personal control, high monetary yields, tax advantages, and accessibility are some of the basic reasons why real estate should be your investment of choice. Those reasons have prevailed for decades, surviving all economic and political conditions. The prognosis for the future? Bright—as long as we are confined to living on this planet with its limited supply of land and its almost unlimited supply of people. Although it took us millions of years to reach a worldwide population of over 5 billion, demographers estimate that by the year 2050 the Earth's population will exceed 10 billion. With that startling news, you've got to admit, real estate will continue to be the source of the most lucrative of investment opportunities.

Long-Term Stability

The IRS, in reporting on the personal net worth of our country's wealthiest individuals, claims that real estate is their most significant listed asset. Why do you suppose that's true? Wealthholders are keenly aware of some important fiscal data. For instance, they know that the purchasing power of money left in savings accounts dissipates with advancing inflation; investments in corporate stocks and bonds fluctuate uncontrollably with every economic and political whim; and local and federal red tape severely increases the risks of opening and operating a small employee-oriented business.

Real estate, on the other hand, is a proven, stable haven in which one can accumulate a steady stream of wealth. From the end of World War II to the present—despite cyclical, temporary setbacks, real estate has continually grown in value nationwide.

Personal Control

The real estate owner is in the position to control assets valued far in excess of his or her invested capital. Through the intelligent use of leverage, a modest down payment can put an investor in control of an asset worth over 10 times the invested capital.

Rather than depending on a financial advisor whose actions may or may not result in your financial gain, as a self-directed real estate investor, you can plot your own path, making your own decisions about what, where, and when to buy or sell.

As an example, I went on a shopping spree for investment houses starting in 1983. At that time, the real estate industry was recovering from earlier massive interest rates of more than 17 percent. A disenchanted public, unable to qualify for real estate loans, created a very sluggish resale market. Houses weren't selling; appreciation temporarily ceased; and lenders were awash with foreclosed properties.

As bad as that period was for ordinary homeowners who needed to sell their properties, for the investor it was a window of opportunity. I, and others like me, bought up as many bank-owned distressed properties as possible.

By the late 1980s, fixed interest rates settled down to around 11 percent and the dormant "appreciation" revived. My properties more than doubled in value. There appeared to be no end to the upward flight of house prices. When I began to calculate my net equities, I felt like I hit the jackpot or won the lottery. It was wonderful!

Then came 1989. The euphoria disappeared. Suddenly the skyrocketing market came to an abrupt standstill. "Now what?" I thought. "Well, how about raising more capital and proceeding with my investment program?" Seizing what proved to be another golden opportunity, I took advantage of the enormous equities I had in my distressed properties and refinanced them. Then, I used the money to purchase a 1.3 acre lot in a very exclusive gated community in Westlake Village, California.

Shortly afterwards, my wife and I engaged a creative architect and quality builder to construct a magnificent $2.5 million estate. When the project is completed and subsequently sold, we expect to net a profit of nearly $900,000 from the venture.

The personal account here is not given boastfully. It's an example of how, as an independent investor, I took advantage of the various housing markets. I didn't wait for someone to egg me on or to "advise" me. I did it on my own, because I knew that a poor real estate market in 1983 was the precursor of a boom and that the enormous equities I held could provide the needed capital to fund another money-making project.

Being able to take the initiative and control my own actions is one of the most appealing features about investing in real estate.

High Monetary Yields

When professional property owners extol the high monetary yields of real estate investing, some financial experts are quick to criticize them. They admit that although the ultimate earnings may be very satisfactory, the nonliquidity of real estate is a viable drawback from its desirability as an investment vehicle. They then cite the case of a friend or neighbor who has been trying to sell a property for more than six months with no takers in sight. I've heard the same story myself. But, the truth is this:

Real estate is nonliquid and remains unsold for long periods of time only when sellers price it beyond its market value.

Many sellers out there pick a number out of the air and say, "This is the price I've got to get for my house"; or, "This price is what the house is worth to me." Both of these declarations are totally invalid. What you "must get" for your house, or "what it's worth to you" may have nothing to do with its true market value.

The nonliquidity of real estate could be curtailed if property owners were to realize that buyers, not sellers, ultimately determine the sale price. Motivated sellers do a market survey to determine the sale price. Armed with that information, they then realistically price their property for a quick sale.

Remember, it's especially foolish to allow investment property to languish on the market for long periods of time.

7

The length of time you hold an investment property before sale influences your yield.

In an investment venture where you buy a distressed property and fix it up for immediate resale—sometimes called "flipping"—the earnings on your investment are adversely affected by making extended monthly mortgage payments to your lender. To avoid that situation I recommend:

1. Know your future net sale price *before* you purchase your property.

2. Buy distressed property for at least 15 to 20 percent below that figure.

3. Price it realistically for a quick sale.

4. Employ an aggressive, knowledgeable real estate agent to properly market the property.

Appreciation and Inflation

A long-term benefit of real estate is not realized until the property is sold. That long-term benefit is *appreciation*, the increase in value that accrues to a property over the passage of time. Although "flipping" property—a quick buy, fix, sell process—produces an immediate monetary return, a much longer holding period is needed to take advantage of appreciation. Of course, while you hold the property, ideally its rental income should meet its holding costs. For those costs not met, however, provided your situation complies with the current IRS guidelines, you may be able to take a deduction from your reportable gross income. More about that later.

Appreciation is the real wealth-building facet of real estate. As I cited earlier, properties I purchased in 1983 more than doubled in value by 1989. That represented an average six-year rate of appreciation of about 12 percent. Yearly appreciation rates are not steady; they fluctuate with the whims of the regional economy. A couple of years in a cycle may show 20 percent rates of appreciation, but another couple of years may show considerably less of an increase. Over the long haul, however, appreciation makes property owners rich.

In speaking about appreciation, you must also address the issue of inflation. Although inflation ultimately erodes purchasing power, appreciation ultimately increases it. Why? Because over a period of time, the rate of appreciation has traditionally exceeded the rate of inflation during that same period, reinforcing the concept that the ownership of real estate is a viable hedge against inflation. It's a real wealth-building advantage for property owners.

To illustrate the effect of inflation and appreciation on the creation of wealth, consider the following contrasting examples:

$10,000 Bank Account Investment

$	10,000	Deposited for one year.
+	500	Reportable 5% interest to the IRS.
−	600	6% inflation rate applied to the $10,000 deposit equals a $600 loss of purchasing power.
−	100	Net loss from 5% interest and 6% inflation.
−	140	$500 reportable interest income creates a tax liability of $140 in the 28% bracket.
$	-240	Total loss on $10,000 savings account.

$10,000 Real Estate Investment

$	10,000	10% down payment on a $100,000 property.
	106,000	Value of $100,000 property after one year with a 6% rate of appreciation.
	6,000	Reportable profit on a sale by owner of $106,000 property without taking into account escrow fees.
−	1,680	Taxes on $6,000 profit at the 28% bracket.
	4,320	Net profit after taxes on $10,000 investment.
−	859	6% inflation reduces the purchasing power of $10,000 invested and $4,320 net profit. (0.06 x 14,320)
$	3,461	Net adjusted return on $10,000 investment = 34.6%.

9

Compare a loss of $240 in a savings account with a $3,461 profit from a real estate investment, and you'll begin to see the tremendous advantage of the real estate investments over bank accounts.

The preceding comparison cited inflation and appreciation at the same yearly rate even though that situation usually is not the case. However, I did that to illustrate that even in that unlikely scenario, real estate wins.

Furthermore, the rate of return for the property owner could increase exponentially if the asset were held through periods of excessively high appreciation. But even at a modest appreciation rate of 6 percent, using the "Rule of 72" calculation, the $100,000 property just cited will double in value to $200,000 in 12 years.

The Rule of 72 is a mathematical function that tells you the number of years it will take a sum of money to double at a certain percentage rate. In this example, divide 72 by 6 (the percentage of appreciation) to arrive at 12, the number of years required for the property's value to double.

As time goes by and buildable land becomes less plentiful, real estate can't help but become more valuable. In some areas of the world, the price for real property is already unreal. Read on.

A 1991 article in the Business Section of the *Los Angeles Times*[1] quoted the National Tax Agency of Japan. It said that agency is currently assessing land in the prestigious Ginza shopping district of Tokyo at the rate of $252,000 per square yard! And, that figure is up 17.5 percent from a year earlier! Just for the fun of it, I calculated that at that rate, the assessed value of a modest 5,000 square foot lot in that area would be $140,000,000. Does that help you understand why the Japanese investors buy so much real estate in the United States? Here, for $140,000,000 they can buy several regional shopping centers or millions of square feet of office space.

Refinancing

Another source of monetary yield from real estate is called refinancing. During my investment career, I constantly used refinance money to raise capital for further purchases. Remember:

It is never wrong to safely increase the loans on your properties to raise cash for additional property purchases.

Refinance capital is tax free; it's not reportable income! In all the distressed properties I've owned, I have taken out via refinance more money—in most cases, significantly more money—than I originally invested.

Use refinancing wisely. Grow rich by borrowing money. Although that may sound like a contradiction of terms it really works. You'll see how it applies to distressed properties in particular later in this book.

Tax Advantages

Despite the 1986 Tax Reform Act, there are still tax advantages to owning real estate. However, forget about considering real estate just as a tax shelter, as was so frequently done in the past. Those days are over. No longer can real estate investment groups lure participants with the promise of limitless write-offs against their ordinary income.

In a way, the revised tax situation may be good. The new law corrected the insane practice of erecting "see-through" office buildings merely as tax dodges, without any rationale for their economic use or necessity. The Resolution Trust Corporation, formed by the U.S. government to sell off failed S&L foreclosed properties, is attempting to unload many of these "tax-dodge" buildings.

The new tax law has some limitations. To take advantage of the write-off possibilities:

1. You must have ownership in the distressed property that exceeds 10 percent.

2. You must materially participate in the operation of your rental properties. That is, you must supervise managers,

employ tradespeople, collect rents—do something that involves you personally.

3. Then the law says you may deduct up to $25,000 of business losses from your ordinary income if it's under $100,000. If it's $100,000 and over, then for every dollar over $100,000 you may deduct 50 cents of loss. When your ordinary income reaches $150,000, the $25,000 write-off is completely eliminated.

Even though the top limitations will seriously erode the write-off capabilities of high-income people, for those earning less than $100,000 the $25,000 deduction could be a formidable income tax savings.

I have never advocated investing in real estate primarily to create a tax write-off.

Although I certainly took advantage of the tax laws as they applied to real estate, that was always the frosting on the cake to me. The wealth-building advantages of investing in real estate have always far exceeded the tax advantages of doing so.

Accessibility

The real estate business is accessible to nearly everyone. If you've been steadily employed and have a good credit record, you are a potential participant. Even if you have little start-up capital, there are ways to work around the lack of cash that I'll describe later.

If you know nothing about real estate investing, the world around you is burgeoning with reliable, pertinent information. Bookstores and libraries have stacks of contemporary works written by practicing professionals. Title companies, local realty boards, mortgage companies, and escrow firms offer informative lectures on various aspects of the subject free of charge. It's all there; yours for the taking! As you begin your career in real estate, I urge you to avail yourself of the plethora of information at hand and learn, learn, learn.

Personality Traits You Need to Buy Distressed Real Estate

As accessible as real estate is to everyone, those with a certain group of personality traits will have the best chance of super success—especially with distressed properties. This section tells you what to look for.

Self-Starter

You must be a doer—someone who makes things happen. The investment opportunities are out there, but they won't announce themselves to you. You have to find them. In order to do that, you must have an intense desire to be in total control of your life; then, you have to harness all the energy necessary to accomplish that control.

Finding one suitable distressed property may take weeks or even months of phone calls, analyses, and rejections. The temptation to quit will rear its ugly head. If it does, you must fight back with even stronger diligence and perseverance. As a self-starter you have no one to look to for direction, encouragement, or advice. All of it—the whole enchilada—has to come from inside you.

Optimist

You have to maintain a positive attitude about the future of real estate. The possibility always exists that you may have a few rough spots to overcome in your quest for financial independence. Sluggish markets, slow-paying tenants, untimely repair bills, vacancies—all

13

those travails and others may happen. They will put your optimism to a severe test. The brooders will give up; the future millionaires will react differently:

They will dwell on a positive thought every time something goes wrong. They will ponder how they're building an enormous estate that will provide them with a lifestyle unmatched by most others. Instead of feeling irate toward a tenant or a clogged toilet, they will think long term; that tenant and clogged toilet are mere stepping stones to their future prosperity.

Just about everyone agrees that an optimistic outlook is beneficial to one's health, wealth, and well-being. Some people come by it naturally; others have to learn it.

A "downer" will accuse an optimist of being blind to reality. But an optimist doesn't bury his or her head in the sand. Although the optimist acknowledges negative events, he or she doesn't dwell on them nor allow them to impede progress. The optimist focuses on the "big picture," the "light at the end of the tunnel," and the "pot of gold at the end of the rainbow." If you're an optimist, you're at least halfway to success in real estate investing.

Courageous

Can you see yourself completely emptying out a large apartment house of good, cash-paying tenants and taking complete charge of converting it into a condominium project? On a smaller scale, do you think you could take hard-earned money from your savings account, use it as a down payment on a trashed-out house, and then work all kinds of hours fixing it for sale or rent? How about this? Buy yourself an apartment house with extensive deferred maintenance, spend loads of capital to improve it, and then as vacancies occur, raise the rents to increase the building's value?

Those are a few of the most popular money-making opportunities in real estate. Unless you have the guts to take on projects like that, to recognize gold where others see trash, you'll reject many of those profitable opportunities.

Organized

No matter how small your operation, you'll have to keep detailed records—if only for the IRS. You'll have to make timely payments to lenders and to tradesmen who work on your properties. If you get into the apartment business, you'll have to train managers to keep their records straight and you'll have to develop a "no nonsense" system of collecting rents and selecting tenants. Chapter 13 details the kinds of information you'll record and provides sample forms for creating your records.

Good organization, to me, even means keeping detailed records of conversations between you and the principals involved in your escrow transactions. Organization dignifies your business and lends enforcement to your self-reliance.

Preparing for Success

This chapter gave you some solid reason why you should invest in distressed real estate. I've pointed out some personality traits you should try to develop to increase your chances of supersuccess in real estate investing.

In the material that follows, we'll get down to specifics and suggest step-by-step procedures to follow so you can duplicate my "win on the way in" distressed real estate deals.

As you read the "how to" formats, pause to think, "I can do this. If Skip did it, I can, too." Repeat this thought to condition yourself to rely on your judgment and to expect success.

The investment ideas presented in this book are not predicated on the occurrence of pie-in-the-sky events. Although some of your transactions may prove to be more involved than others, they're all basic, down-to-earth deals concluded daily all across America by people just like you.

Let's go!

[1]*Los Angeles Times,* January 23, 1991, Section D, p. 2.

Selecting Your First Distressed Property

This chapter shows you the best type of marked-down property to start with in your quest for distressed real estate, then gives you a step-by-step guide for finding a likely property right in your neighborhood and making a profitable deal when you buy it.

Single Family, Entry-Level Rental Houses: Best Bet for Beginners

In the real estate environment of the mid-1990s, the best bet for a freshman investor is the purchase of a distressed, entry-level single family house.

"Entry-level" describes property affordable by first-time homebuyers—the largest segment of the real estate market. It also means property affordable by the greatest number of house renters. Of course, you can make money by purchasing and refurbishing distressed property to rent or sell in any price range. However, for the beginner, it's best to stick with the entry-level category, because the costs are more manageable.

Besides offering invaluable self-training that can be applied later toward the purchase and operation of apartment houses or commercial properties, the single family rental offers you the following advantages:

- Nonowner-occupied single family rentals are relatively easy to finance and refinance—although at one time they were resisted by lenders.

- Single family house rentals are in great demand.

- Rental houses are normally exempt from rent control ordinances.

- House renters move about less frequently, thus creating longer, more stable tenancies.

- House renters tend to be less abusive of property than apartment dwellers.

- Appreciation creates a great deal of unearned wealth for house owners.

- Single family, low-end homes are relatively easy to sell, making them a more liquid investment than an apartment house.

- The value of an apartment house is predicated primarily on its income. Not so for single family houses; their value is based solely on sales of comparable dwellings in their neighborhood.

- It takes less capital to buy and rehab a house than an apartment building.

- It takes less "know-how" to buy and operate a single family rental than an apartment house.

Now that you know the advantages of purchasing a distressed entry-level, single family house as your first real estate venture, the rest of the section suggests how you go about it:

1. Locate for possible purchase a lower-priced distressed property in a good neighborhood.

2. Approach the purchase as if you were going to sell immediately after rehab (even though your plan may be to rent the property out and hold on to it for future appreciation).

3. Determine your future net sale price *before* you purchase the property.

Precalculating Your Profits

Finding the future net sale price of a property before you purchase it is relatively easy. Some leg work and a few phone calls are all it takes. However, easy as it may be, it is absolutely crucial in order to orchestrate a money-making deal. Here's what you can do.

1. Discover comparable sale prices in the area. Call the customer service office of a local title company and request a property profile on your proposed purchase (the legal description of the property, the name of the legal owner, the outstanding loans, and other pertinent data) and comparable properties sold recently in the area.

2. Knowing the size and amenities of your proposed purchase, ask local real estate agents what that type of property in top condition has been going for in the neighborhood.

3. When you have the sales comps in hand, visit each one and find the comparable style and size of home in tip-top condition that matches closest to the run-down model you may purchase.

4. After finding your model comparable, from its sale price, deduct 6 percent for the probable real estate commission and 1 percent for possible *escrow fees*. This is the *net sale price*— the price you will probably net when you sell your property after rehab.

19

Escrow fees is the catch-all term that encompasses all of the administrative costs involved in the transfer or refinancing of a property. Depending on the transaction, any of the following items could be included in escrow fees:

• Prorated taxes

• Accrued interest

• Title insurance

• County and city transfer taxes

• Reconveyance and recording fees

• Demand and cancellation fees

• Loan process and tax service fees

• Escrow company fees

Escrow fees vary by state and even by town. For my deals in Southern California, I use 1 percent of the sale price as the probable cost of escrow fees. However, Los Angeles has recently imposed a transfer tax on all real estate sales, so in my future deals I will increase the escrow percentage I must deduct.

If in your area the escrow fees (or closing costs, or whatever your local terminology is) are higher than 1 percent, you must deduct the costs from the sale price in calculating your profits. If you've had no experience with these costs, talk with real estate agents or others who are involved with the transfer of properties to learn what the usual percentage is. Many areas have escrow companies or title companies that handle the transfer of property. Other areas use attorneys.

Later you'll learn about the Real Estate Settlement Procedures Act. It guarantees that buyers obtain more information about escrow fees prior to real estate closings.

5. Structure the purchase so that you will make a minimum of 40 percent profit on all funds expended—down payment and holding costs included.

In order to achieve that minimum of 40 percent profit, test the property you're considering with the following questions:

1. Will I be able to purchase the distressed property for at least 15 percent below the net sale price of the best comparable property in the immediate neighborhood?

2. Will I be able to purchase the property with no more than 10 percent down?

3. Will my sale price after renovation match or exceed that of the best comparable?

4. Will 5 percent of the projected sale price be enough to cover the costs of rehabilitation?

5. Will my holding period from the close of purchase escrow to the close of sale escrow (or a signed rental agreement if I intend to hold on to the property for future appreciation) be four months or less?

Answering yes to all five questions on the test means your property is likely to be a good deal.

To purchase property with just 10 percent down implies 90 percent financing. If you intend to live on the property, a loan in the amount of 90 percent of the appraised value of the property is possible. However, for any loan in an amount of 90 percent of more of the appraised value, you'll have to pay for private mortgage insurance (PMI). PMI insures the lender against financial loss if the borrower fails to make the required payments. The annual premium is small—about one-half of 1 percent of the loan amount.

If you don't intend to live on the property, securing 90 percent financing in a single loan will be a problem. You may not be able to find a lender for that kind of loan in today's financial climate. For a nonowner-occupied property, your best loan may be for 80 percent of the appraised value. If that proves to be the case, you must ask the seller to help finance the deal.

As a contingency of sale, ask the seller to "take back" a second trust deed for the difference between the first trust deed and the sale price, less your 10 percent down payment.

To take back (or "carry back") a second trust deed means that the seller lends the buyer a portion of *equity* (ownership value) in the

21

property for a certain length of time. The security for this loan is a trust deed that the seller records or files with the county. This is called a "second" trust deed, because it comes behind the previously recorded first deed.

For example assume the sale price and the bank's appraised value for your property are the same. With a $150,000 purchase and 10 percent down, you'll end up with two trust deeds—a first for $120,000 and a second for $15,000.

First and Second Trust Deeds for $150,000 Property

$	150,000	Sale price
–	15,000	Down payment
	135,000	Amount to finance
–	120,000	80% first trust deed or mortgage
$	15,000	Second trust deed or mortgage

The first lender to consider when you purchase a property is the lender now holding the first trust deed or mortgage that the seller has. Ask that institution whether it will give you the loan you want.

Before we continue, take a moment to understand the distinction between the seldom-used financing instrument known as a mortgage and the more popular trust deed.

A *mortgage* is a two-party instrument that consists of an agreement between the lender (mortgagee) and the borrower (mortgagor). With a mortgage, title to the property rests with the mortgagor subject to the lien in favor of the lender, or mortgagee.

A *trust deed* is a three-party instrument that includes the lender (beneficiary), the borrower (trustor), and the custodian of the title (trustee). Title to the property passes from the trustee to the trustor when the trustor pays off the loan.

There are some other differences between a mortgage and a trust deed in terms of the foreclosure process, but you'll learn more about that later.

Lenders always base the percentage of their loan amount on their appraised value of the property and not the sale price.

If the appraised value of a property is less than your purchase price and the seller doesn't agree to a price reduction, either the seller must carry back a larger second trust deed, or you must come up with a larger down payment—or you can split the difference.

Financing When the Sale Price Exceeds Appraised Value

$	145,000	Appraised value
	150,000	Sale price
–	116,000	80% loan
$	34,000	Difference between sale price and loan amount
–	17,000	Down payment
$	17,000	Amount required in second trust deed
or		
$	34,000	Difference between sale price and loan amount
–	15,000	10% down payment
$	19,000	Amount required in second trust deed

Let's say you have identified an entry-level distressed property in a nice, modest neighborhood. From your drive-by inspection, it appears as though the property's deferred maintenance may be easily addressed—only creative cosmetic changes are needed to make the home fit in with the well-kept ones around it.

Further investigations reveal another home—one that is well-kept—that closely resembles the distressed property. You find from recent *comps*—listings of similar properties sold recently—that this type of home sold for about $185,000 when its condition was good.

23

Thus, you can reason that if you can buy the rundown version for a low enough price, you'll be able to make some money here. You proceed with the next step: the inspection.

Inspection

Now, you're ready to intimately inspect your subject property to accurately compare it with the comparable. You ask:

"What is the extent of its deferred maintenance? How much will it cost to bring it up to a $185,000 sale price?"

To help you remember what to inspect during your tour, use the Checklist for Inspecting a Single Family Property.

Checklist for Inspecting a Single Family Property

Interior

Yes	No	Item
___	___	Do all the appliances work?
___	___	Do the heating and air conditioning work properly?
___	___	Is the electrical system adequate?
___	___	Do all the plumbing fixtures and piping work properly?
___	___	Are telephone lines and jacks up to date?
___	___	Are walls and ceilings smooth and free of leaks and stains?
___	___	Are floors in good repair?
___	___	Are carpeting and window treatments free of wear and stains?
___	___	Are all light fixtures operational?

Exterior

___	___	Is the landscaping attractive?
___	___	Is the foundation sound?
___	___	Is brick free of loose mortar and siding free of buckles and dents?
___	___	Are doors and windows in good repair and airtight?
___	___	Are downspouts, gutters, soffits, and fascia leakfree and adequate for storm runoffs?
___	___	Is the roof in good condition?

If you feel that you lack experience in conducting inspections, it may behoove you to hire a professional building inspector for the job. For a modest fee, the house inspector will prepare a detailed list of all the property's deficiencies, many of which might escape you. A statement about the condition of the property prepared by a disinterested third party will help you negotiate with the seller, as well.

Throughout this book, I advocate buying entry-level property "as is"—in other words, in its current state without any warranties from the seller. That means that you, the buyer, assume all the risks. But it's your acceptance of those risks that can persuade the seller to deal with you. You must make it easy for the seller to dispose of a problem-ridden property that he or she apparently can't maintain. The inspection report, therefore, is used as your bargaining tool to give credence to your lowball offer. It shouldn't be used to force the seller to improve property he or she already can't maintain.

Revising Your Numbers

After the completion of the inspection, consult tradespeople for the various costs of repairs. Those contractors won't be able to give you exact numbers, but they will give you ballpark estimates. If the property needs draperies, carpeting or new appliances, research the best price available for those items.

The optimum situation is where the cost of rehabilitation will not exceed 5 percent of your projected sale price of $185,000. If it does exceed 5 percent, you should adjust your purchase price downward accordingly.

Because the best-priced comparable property in your area sold for a gross price of $185,000, try to bring your rehabbing costs in at about $9,250, which is 5 percent of $185,000.

Knowing the gross sale price of $185,000, you can now easily determine that your probable net sale price will be $172,050 ($185,000 less 11,100, which is 6 percent real estate commission and $1,850, which is 1 percent possible escrow fees).

After computing the net sale price figure, you can now determine the possible price range of your purchase. Remember, you have to buy for at least 15 to 20 percent below the comparable's net sale price of $172,050 in order to ensure a decent profit. In this case, that means you'd have to pay between $138,000 (a 20 percent discount) and $146,000 (a 15 percent discount) for your distressed model.

Armed with the knowledge of a profitable purchase price range, you now have to go back to your records and reexamine the "ballpark" costs of rehabilitation that you gathered earlier. If those numbers added up to more than $9,250—5 percent of the $185,000 projected sale price—you will have to stick very close to a purchase price discount of 20 percent. If they didn't, you may have a little more leeway in your purchase negotiations.

To get on with our sample transaction, assume you and the seller ultimately compromised on a purchase price of $142,000, with 10 percent down. You determined that your rehabbing costs will be about $9,250—meeting the 5 percent benchmark figure. By doing that intensive a rehabilitation, you feel you'll be able to get at least $185,000 for the property when you sell.

With the compilation of that information, the property has now passed the test for four of the five questions about profitability. You're well on your way to a good money-making deal:

1. Will I be able to purchase the distressed property for at least 15 percent below the net sale price of the best comparable property in the immediate neighborhood?
    Answer: Yes, $142,000.

2. Will I be able to purchase the property with no more than 10 percent down? *Answer:* Yes, $14,200.

3. Will my sale price after renovation match or exceed that of the best comparable? *Answer:* Yes, $185,000.

4. Will 5 percent of the projected sale price be enough to cover the costs of rehabilitation? *Answer:* Yes, $9,250.

Now you're ready to pursue the answer to the last question: Will my holding period from the close of purchase escrow to the close of sale escrow (or a signed rental agreement if I intend to hold on to the property for future appreciation) be four months or less?

After you complete the rehab, with luck in about four weeks, the property is ready to rent or sell. If you're going to sell, the house should be in what real estate people call "turnkey" condition. That means that all the prospective buyer will have to do is turn the key, open the door, and move in. You can get away with some rehab shortcuts if you plan to rent the property out. But if you plan to sell, spend the extra dollars and make the property perfect. You'll find that entry-level properties that are tastefully decorated—the properties that dazzle—sell the fastest even in today's sluggish market.

Don't be greedy! You'll be tempted to price your property for more than your best comps, because you'll feel yours is better and more attractively decorated. Be careful. Give lots of credence to what real estate agents told you and what the comps revealed.

Don't overprice the property. This deal is not your retirement fund. You don't have to make a killing!

It's better to price your property competitively, make the sale, and go on to your next project. Waiting around for another few thousand dollars ultimately costs you dearly.

Entry-level homes in turnkey condition in good neighborhoods sell under almost any market condition. There's always someone out there ready and willing to buy that kind of property, especially with today's attractive interest rates for loans.

It's wiser business practice to price the property to sell now rather than overprice it, cool your heels for several months with the property unsold, and then lower the price to what it should have been in the first place.

Here are some tips I've used to move property in today's slow market:

1. Find yourself a "go-getter" real estate agent.

2. Price the house for sale, not ego.

3. Present the house in as fine a condition as possible.

4. Insist that the agent advertise your property every weekend or offer to share the cost of doing so.

27

5. Increase showings of the property by offering a bonus to the agent who sells the home—the bonus could be cash (about $250), a VCR, or a weekend at a nice resort.

6. For any open house, have coffee brewing. Offer it to callers. It's a nice gesture and the aroma makes people linger to see the improvements you've made.

7. Create color brochures featuring an attractive picture of your house. Your callers can "take your house home with them."

8. Hold a "broker's open house." Professional agents are invited and given refreshments. By previewing the property, they'll feel more comfortable subsequently showing it to prospects.

9. Have all callers fill out a name card and drop it into a bowl. At the end of the month, have a drawing and give the winner $100.

Using these marketing ideas, my properties have sold in less than four months. So we'll assume that our sample property does likewise. In order to determine in advance what your holding costs will be, you'll have to construct the probable purchase transaction.

Purchase Transaction

$	142,000	Purchase price
–	14,200	10% down payment
	127,800	Balance of purchase price to be financed
–	2,170	1½ points plus $250 in loan fees added to the purchase price balance
$	129,970	New 8% adjustable rate loan for 30 years with payments of about $954 per month

Four-Month Holding Costs

$	3,816	(4 × $954) total mortgage payments
+	480	(4 × $120) estimated total real estate taxes
+	100	(4 × $25) estimated total insurance
$	4,396	Total holding costs

With all these numbers at hand, you'll be able to see the outcome of a sale of this property for $185,000.

Sale of the Property

Figuring Proceeds:

$	185,000	Sale price
−	12,950	7% costs of sale (1% escrow and 6% to a broker)
	172,050	Net sale price
−	129,970	Loan balance
$	42,080	Net proceeds from sale

Figuring Cash Invested:

$	14,200	Down payment
+	9,250	Rehab costs
+	4,396	Holding costs
+	1,420	Original purchase escrow fees
$	29,266	Total spent

Figuring Profit:

$	42,080	Net proceeds from sale
	29,266	Total spent
$	12,814	Profit

By dividing the profit of $12,814 by the $29,266 cash invested, you find the investment earned approximately 44 percent in just four months from the close of purchase escrow to the close of sale escrow.

Let's take a "worse-case" scenario and see what results in this deal if, despite our best efforts, the property sells in six months rather than four. How does that affect our profit?

- The holding period costs rise from $4,396 to $6,594.

- The profit drops from $12,814 to $10,616.

- The profit percentage drops from 44 percent to 34 percent—still not small potatoes!

Are you still pondering the question, "Why should I invest in real estate?" How many other investments have netted you 44 percent return in four months or 34 percent in six?

The best time to buy anything is when all your competition is selling; the best time to sell is when your product is in short supply and you have lots of eager buyers. As a real estate entrepreneur, you operate as a buyer *and* a seller. By keeping alert and being sensitive to the world of real estate around you, you can make money in either a buyer's or seller's market.

Mining the Gold in Your Neighborhoods

You now know the best type of distressed real estate you should buy and are acquainted with the important guidelines that should assure you of a good deal. This section gives you the step-by-step application of those guidelines in a practical situation. But first, let me share a little story.

I bought a beat-up house in a lovely tract of modest homes overlooking a canyon. Besides its bright, airy kitchen, the home had three bedrooms, two baths, a family room, and a living room, for a total of about 1,275 square feet. When I completed the rehab, the house looked beautiful.

I held my first open house on a balmy Sunday afternoon. One of my first visitors was the neighbor directly across the street. He said he had to come over and take a look. As he walked through the home, I knew he liked what he saw. As he turned to leave, he said, "You know, this house sat here in its sorry state for months. I had the opportunity and the money to buy it, but I didn't. I thought about it a lot, but I did nothing. I'm a school teacher. I probably could have made more money investing in this property than I made all year teaching."

Other neighbors, too, said that the golden opportunity for this property slipped right through their fingers. Learn from their mistake! To find an entry-level distressed house in your neighborhood takes little effort. It's probably the easier investment project to accomplish. Chapter 3 shows you some other wonderful sources of distressed properties.

Step 1.   Find Your Investment Property

Location has always been and still is the most important element in a good real estate deal. You cannot evade nor skirt that fact. For the beginning investor, finding a property in a good location is the most crucial factor in culminating a profitable deal.

My definition of *distressed property,* you'll recall, excluded real estate located in hostile environments. No matter what you do to improve a distressed property in such a neighborhood, you won't reap the same benefits as you would in a stable one. The environment is too overwhelming and intense for a beginning entrepreneur to handle. Such areas have to be improved by massive government-assisted redevelopment programs that are beyond the realm of freshman investors.

Therefore, if you live in an area with serious socioenvironmental problems, my first suggestion is to find your closest neighborhood of modest, well-kept homes and target that area for your first deal. Look for a neighborhood of nice, entry-level housing that's affordable for newlyweds and young professionals. Whether you sell or rent, they'll be the source of your most qualified customers.

Even if you live in a wealthy or upper-middle-class neighborhood, you should pursue your first distressed real estate deal out of your immediate area. You, too, should find the neighborhood closest to you that features modest, entry-level housing and concentrate there.

In all my years in real estate, distressed entry-level housing has always been my investment of choice. I've bought in all kinds of safe, well-kept neighborhoods—some whose population was predominantly white, some predominantly black, and some predominantly Hispanic—and did very well. Stick to the rules; rely on the tips in this book and you should do very well, too.

After you've located your neighborhood of choice, drive up and down each street and write down the address of every house that appears to need some serious tender loving care. Look for cosmetic deficiencies only, not structural damage.

Here are some sample clues for detecting distressed properties:

- The landscape is overgrown and the lawn is weedy.

- Window screens are torn and hanging loose from the house.

- The paint is faded and peeling.

- The driveway is laced with cracks.

- There's an accumulation of junk all over the place.

- There are shingles missing from the roof.

- There are cracked windows.

- It looks abandoned.

If you have a Polaroid camera, take a picture of each distressed property for future reference.

Step 2. Locate the Owners and Arrange to Inspect the Home

When you get home, call your county office center and ask for the names and addresses of the owners of each distressed property you observed. Then, write the owners the following note:

> Hi, my name is Tom Smith. I'm interested in buying your house "as is" at _____.

> If you'd like to sell it to me now or in the near future, please call me at _____. Hope to hear from you.

> P.S. This isn't a solicitation for a listing. I'm not a real estate agent.

Chances are, if you send enough owners this message, you'll elicit some positive responses. However, not every owner of a distressed property wants to sell. A poignant reality is the fact that many cash-starved owners of maintenance-deficient properties who do want to sell, simply can't. Buyers for run-down real estate are hard to find. To those owners, your little note may be manna from heaven.

It's true: One person's problem can be another person's opportunity.

To those homeowners who respond positively to your note, call and make an appointment to immediately inspect their property and gather needed information. Ask the owners to contact each lender on the property and have the following information available to you:

- Is the note assumable?
- If so, what are the costs and terms?
- Will the current lenders refinance the property for a buyer?
- If so, what are the costs and terms?
- Do any of the notes have a prepayment penalty?
- Are there any other liens against the property, such as a mechanic's lien or an IRS lien?

On your inspection tour, write down, room by room and all around the outside, all the deferred maintenance you'll have to correct using the Checklist for Inspecting a Single Family Property, listing everything from leaky faucets to dingy draperies and carpeting. Do the same kind of meticulous inspection of the garage. At the completion of your inspection tour, say goodbye to your hosts and make another appointment to see them. Give yourself about five working days. You'll need that time to prepare yourself because at the next meeting you're going to make them an offer.

Step 3. Find Out About the Property

Take my advice: *Always* learn as much about a property as possible before you make an offer. Then, purchase it as if you were going to immediately sell it, even if you wind up renting it out.

How do you research your prospective properties? It's easy; most of it involves phone calls. To begin with, call a local title company and ask for a "property profile." It's usually free of charge and contains the following information:

- The legal owners' names and address

- Outstanding liens

- A plat map showing the lot's location, its dimensions, and easements, if any

- The property's legal description

- Sales comparables (must be specifically requested) going back no more than one year

By having the recent sales comps, which are the recent sales prices of similar properties in the targeted area, you can

1. Estimate your future net sales price, as described earlier.

2. Determine what your purchase price must be in order to ensure a respectable profit.

Although it will be uncovered by a title search in escrow, it's a good idea to call the county tax collector to find out if there are any unpaid property taxes. If there are, you'll be able to use that information in negotiating your price.

Step 4. Revisit the Neighborhood

After you receive your property profile and comparable properties' sales prices, go back to the neighborhood and compare those homes to your prospective purchase. Will the improvements you decided to do be sufficient to make the property saleable at a price equal to or exceeding the sales prices of your comps? Be careful. You can lose money by overimproving a property. In other words, if you're in a Chevrolet neighborhood, don't improve your property to the Cadillac level.

The level of refurbishing that will yield the greatest return on your investment is the level shown in the majority of your best comps. Don't unnecessarily upgrade your property's amenities, because that's not likely to result in a higher sale price.

It's cheaper to clean and restore existing appliances and fixtures rather than to replace them. If they're in good shape and respond to a good scrubbing, go for it.

Another caveat: Time is money. Try to keep your refurbishing time down to four weeks. You've got to begin the sale process as soon as possible to keep your holding costs in line. If the refurbishing period will exceed four weeks, you should buy the property for a lower price.

In "casing" your comps, take detailed notes about the quality of their amenities. In the interior, what kind of carpeting, draperies, kitchen appliances, plumbing, and electrical fixtures do they have? In your rehab, try to *match* quality but *outdo* good taste. Don't waste money on upgrades that are out of sync with the neighborhood.

For instance, if your comps feature nice, average-quality nylon carpeting, don't exceed the comps by installing $40-a-yard Berber in your place; if comps have adequate ready-made window coverings, don't install custom-made valanced draperies in yours; you don't need Kohler plumbing fixtures if the less-expensive Delta is used in your comps. Get the idea?

In landscaping, my rule is, less is best. Try to use what's there and make it better. Plants are expensive—don't wantonly dig them up and discard them. Landscapers should concentrate on reshaping the existing trees and shrubbery, cleaning out neglected flower beds, adding color plants, and increasing lawn area wherever possible.

I take two exceptions to decorating when it comes to imitating comps: wallpaper and color.

Some comps may feature several rooms that contain wallpaper. Although I've had some success using it, I've used it sparingly, say for one wall of a dining area. Why is this? Besides being expensive, wallpaper usually doesn't assist a sale. The decision-making, home-purchasing customers are women. I don't think they'd ever agree with me about wallpaper color and pattern choices; thus, I avoid the situation.

Some comps feature a cavalcade of rooms painted in the owner's favorite colors. Don't imitate them! Keep all your rooms the same color—it makes the house look bigger and keeps painting costs down.

You can decorate your properties in any color you want—as long as it's off-white! To indulge your own color fantasies is a mistake.

I have found off-white to be the color of least resistance by most prospective buyers.

Again, some homeowners express personal color preferences in their carpeting. When it comes down to selecting your property's carpet, stick with the currently popular light, neutral earth tones.

Don't entertain self-indulgence when it comes to selecting colors for your rehabs. Stick with colors, patterns, and taste that are generally acceptable.

Don't structurally add or alter anything. Take what's there and make it beautiful. You're not in the remodeling business—that's for carpenters. Your main objective is to make your house a model of the best there is in the neighborhood.

Now that you know what to do when you reexamine the property and plan the improvements, you're ready to take the plunge and make an offer.

Step 5. Prepare Your Offer for at Least 15 Percent Under Market

Prepare your offer for the owners. Let's say recent comparables in the area showed a sale price of $165,000 for a similar house in top condition. That means that an owner will net, after realty and escrow fees, about $153,000. Your price for the distressed model must be no higher than $130,000, a 15 percent discount.

Call the owners and set up a meeting. Tell them you are bringing them an offer. Do not divulge your offer over the phone.

To handle the administrative details of your purchase, one of your first business contacts should be an escrow company, attorney, or title company, depending on the customs of your area. When you prepare your offer, these organizations and individuals may have their own form you can use or can direct you to where you can purchase one.

Although it's customary to present an offer with an earnest money deposit check (often in the amount of 3 percent of the offer, but the figure varies with geography), the check should never be made payable to the sellers. It should be made payable to the entity handling the administrative details. State laws govern the disposition of an earnest money deposit. In the event your deal runs into trouble, you don't want the sellers to have unilateral control of your money.

Step 6. Present Your Offer

Here's how to justify the $130,000 price to the owners:

1. Remind them that if they put the property on the market in its current state, it'll take almost a year to sell. The general public does not buy distressed property. Because the owners lack the money to make the property salable, you're willing to take it off their hands as is.

2. Show them the comparables of properties like theirs that are in top condition.

3. Tell them that the cost of the improvements needed to bring their property up to the sale price level equal to that of the comps is "X" number of dollars. Explain this in detail; the more the better. Always take the high end of the costs for improvements, because you don't yet know how much the repairs will be. In reality, although you should over-

state the approximate costs of correcting the property's deficiencies to the sellers, you must remember that to ensure an adequate profit, you must try to keep those costs down to no more than 5 percent of the sale price.

4. Explain that if the owners sell to you, they'll have no realty commission to pay. On a $165,000 sale, the savings would be as much as $9,900 (6 percent of the sale price).

5. Explain that if the owners sell to you now, there will be a quick escrow and they'll save the cost of many monthly note payments normally incurred waiting for a sale under conventional circumstances.

6. Inform the owners that because you're buying the property from them "as is," you're assuming all the risks—seen and unseen. Explain that you never know just how bad the deficiencies are until you start correcting them.

7. Tell the owners that in order for you to purchase their property "as is," you must be assured of a reasonable profit as payment for the incredible risk you're taking!

8. Then offer them $130,000 (or less)! Have a deposit slip ready made payable to your selected escrow company in the amount of 3 percent of your offer, or $3,900.

9. Write in your offer that you are buying under the following conditions: Your ability to acquire acceptable financing and your approval of the title report and CC & Rs.

CC & Rs is the shortened version of covenants, conditions, and restrictions. With only slight differences in their meanings, they all appear in the land's original grant deed, and they all limit in some way the property's use. "This property may not be used for the keeping of cattle"; "No intoxicating beverages may be sold on this property" are two examples of CC & Rs. Because they're in the original grant deed, they "run with the land." That is, these CC & Rs transfer from owner to owner in perpetuity. However, if a grant deed has a CC & R that restricts the civil rights of a citizen, it is unenforceable.

The CC & Rs are part of your title report. You should examine them to ensure that there are no unusual limitations for your use of the property.

Chances are very good that if you uncover enough properties and send out enough letters, you'll find yourself a good money-making deal. Try it! Follow the procedure I've outlined here. Then after you reap a nice profit from your sale, you don't have to thank me. Just smile all the way to the bank.

Truthfully, after you get started, if you don't make money in real estate, don't blame it on real estate. You're just not trying hard enough! The kind of deal just explained is feasible. Take the necessary time to locate the best property at the lowest price. If your own neighborhood has been totally rehabbed and priced beyond your affordability, check the other sources of distressed properties described in Chapter 3. And don't quit until you find sellers willing to accept your offer. What's more incredible, you can work such deals with little cash. Chapter 4 tells you how.

Sources of Hot Buys

One of the best perks of being in the distressed real estate business is that you can set your own agenda. You can decide just how much you want to accomplish in any particular time period. That's possible because the opportunities to enrich your life are so abundant— they're everywhere. You can't possibly exhaust all the sources of great distressed property buys.

In this chapter, I reveal sources of distressed real estate that have provided me with some of the hottest deals I ever made. I hope that after you examine them, you'll take the initiative to pursue them and profit by them.

REOs: Lender-Owner Real Estate

Real estate owned by banks, S&Ls, and other lenders, commonly known as REOs, can be an important source of great buys of distressed housing. In the past couple of recessionary years so many foreclosures have taken place that lenders are awash with un- wanted houses. It's not unusual to buy property from them very cheaply and sometimes with nothing down.

REOs are an embarrassment to lenders. They normally do not advertise the fact that they have such properties. To find out about REOs, call various lending institutions and ask for their assets owned department.

Another method for locating REOs is to track trustee sales. Trustee sales are published in community and metropolitan newspapers well in advance of the actual sale date. When the sale date elapses, you can call the trustee or the lender. The phone number of at least one of those entities should be given in the sale notice; ask for the asset owned department. Inquire whether the particular property sold at the sale. If it didn't you may have a chance of purchasing it from the lender directly, with favorable financing.

REOs provide you with one of the best sources of distressed discount housing available. Later in this book, you'll learn exactly how to purchase an REO.

Real Estate Agents

It's a good idea to know as many prominent real estate agents as possible. By "prominent," I mean agents whose names are the most conspicuous in a particular area. For instance

For Sale by Ajax Realty

Call Jim Jones

Well, if you see Jim's name more than anyone else's on signs around the neighborhood, chances are he's the area's top producer.

Give your name and phone number to Jim and every other top real estate salesperson in each area in which you'd like to invest. Tell those agents what you're looking for and you can be sure that as soon as a distressed property comes on the market, you'll be contacted.

In dealing with your real estate agent, *never* divulge the highest price you'd be willing to pay for a property. Your agent, most likely, belongs to the National Association of Realtors, and according to its Standard Practice rule 22-1, he or she must reveal that information to the seller's agent. Why? Because the seller, not the buyer, pays the commissions. Therefore, although your agent represents you, he or she is in fact working for the seller, the source of the commission.

Legal Newspapers

Legal newspapers are issued daily or weekly to announce pending litigation and provide legal notice of all types of court cases. These papers are listed in the Yellow Pages of your metropolitan phone directory under the heading "Newspapers." You can use these publications for three types of information: default notices, trustee sales, and divorce or probate cases.

Default Notices

Of particular interest to the real estate entrepreneur are the notices of default, the first stage of a lender's foreclosure action. By learning the details of the foreclosure laws of your state, you can track down some excellent deals well in advance of the involvement of a realty company. Remember, however, that financing your deal can pose a problem if you're not prepared.

Always have an alternate source of financing available in case the lender involved in the foreclosure action chooses not to refinance the property.

43

When you deal with default notices, you have to communicate directly with the people who are on the brink of losing their property. Later I explain the intricacies of the foreclosure process, when to buy in that process, and how to deal with the people facing such a calamity.

If you find coping with people in default emotionally trying, you can wait for the next stage of the foreclosure process, called the trustee sale. At the trustee sale, you deal only with the trustee's representative, not the owners of the property.

Trustee Sale

Trustee sales, the final stage of foreclosure actions, are also published in professional journals. However, to buy at a trustee sale, you must have enough money available to pay off the lender's defaulted loan, the property's accrued penalties, and foreclosure fees. In other words, you need a lot of personal cash—not a very smart way to invest in real estate.

To the entrepreneur, the real value of the trustee sale notice is not the notice itself, but the fact that you can trace the property to the offended lender.

Those properties that don't sell at the trustee sale—and many don't—become the unwanted possessions of the lender, be it a bank, an S&L, or a private party. Those properties are called REOs, as described earlier in the chapter. By immediately contacting the lender, you can purchase these properties at a significant discount, with little or no down payment, and with very attractive financing terms.

Divorce and Probate

Also published in professional journals are divorce filings and probate sales. I'm not a great believer in one's ability to get a real good real estate investment deal at a probate sale—mainly because those properties must be sold at 90 percent of their appraised value. Divorce filings, however, are another possible source of discount housing. If you offer the separating parties a quick "as-is" sale, before they put the property in the hands of a real estate agent, you could possibly achieve an excellent deal.

Local Seat of Government

Your local seat of government is a virtual gift box of potential house bargains. Why? Because certain real estate involved events are recorded there—events such as deaths, divorce, and foreclosure. Those notices are all part of the public record, and no matter how you spell them, they all mean the same thing: opportunities in real estate.

In almost any death or divorce action, there's likely to be some distressed real estate that must be sold off. Through the use of a simple letter or phone call, you can make an appointment to learn whether there indeed is such a situation. If there is, I suggest you follow the process of preparing a bid as outlined in Chapter 2. As long as you reach the divorcing owners before they engage a real estate agent, or as long as the property of a deceased owner does not have to go through probate, you have a good chance of making a profitable as-is purchase.

Another important source of hot buys is the county tax sale. Tax sales occur when property taxes go unpaid for a number of years. The county seizes the parcel of property and is content to sell it for only the taxes due—without regard for its true value.

The proper bidding procedure varies from state to state. Learn how it works in your area; you may be very glad you did! Write a letter to the tax collector of each county in which you have an investment interest. In the letter, ask the collector's office to notify you of the date and locale of each property to be auctioned. The notices you receive will give you the bidding procedure.

When you receive your answer from the tax collector's office, you'll have much work to do before you can proceed to bid. Remember, tax sales do not extinguish mortgage liens. So, even if you "buy" the property from the county for only its taxes due, you may still have to cope with its mortgages, if any exist.

To uncover any mortgages, order a title report or a property profile from a title company. Either document will list outstanding liens, among other things. At the same time you order a title report or profile, order some comparable sales lists. Then, you can do a proper market analysis of the area before you bid.

Again, I remind you: No matter how you acquire your investment property, you must buy for at least 15 percent below your future net sale price in order to make money.

Resolution Trust Corporation (RTC)

In August 1989 Congress created the Resolution Trust Corporation in order to sell off the assets of failed thrifts. Why did the thrifts fail? Bad investments, bad loans, the impact of the 1986 Tax Reform Act, and the recession. More specifically, the trouble was magnified by the excesses of the 1980s: junk bonds; a glut of office buildings, apartment houses, and shopping centers (all competing for the same dwindling supply of tenants); an increase in foreclosures because of the recession; the removal of some tax perks for investment real estate; and poor management. Those are some of the principal reasons for the collapse of many heretofore stalwart institutions.

The RTC now comprises more than 7,000 staff, has 15 regional offices nationwide, and controls over $150 billion in assets—everything from single family homes to huge office complexes. Most of the RTC's properties lie in a belt spreading from Florida to Arizona. But, the corporation does have foreclosed houses just about everywhere.

When the RTC first started to sell real estate, it operated under a Congressional mandate that said all property must be sold at no less than 95 percent of its appraised value. The intention of Congress at the time was to prevent the "dumping" of massive amounts of property on an already depressed real estate market.

However, that ruling has been changed; the differences between market value and appraised value got out of hand, resulting in too few sales. Now, the RTC has the authority to discount prices up to 20 percent below the appraised value. And, if the property doesn't sell in six months, the RTC can discount it another 20 percent!

How do you gain access to the RTC's properties to take advantage of some of these deals? Call the RTC Information Center at 1-800-431-0600. The customer representatives will place you on their mailing list and open up a cornucopia of hot real estate deals for you.

The lists they'll send you will state each asset's identification number, its address, a brief description of it, its price, and the RTC branch office to contact.

When you purchase from the RTC, you do so under the following conditions:

- You must present your offer, with the property ID number, to the proper contact office.

- You must send an earnest money deposit in the amount of 5 percent of your offering bid.

- While the RTC prefers all cash and expects buyers to secure their own financing, they will, under special circumstances, provide financing for you.

- You must buy the property "as is" without any expressed or implied warranty from the RTC.

Again, I must warn you to be careful. The mere fact that you may purchase property from the RTC does not lessen the importance of doing all the proper homework to ensure a profitable venture.

For the convenience of the purchaser, the RTC has a free booklet entitled "How to Buy Property from the Resolution Trust Corporation." It explains the bidding process and can be obtained by writing to the RTC Public Reading Room, 801 17th St. NW, Washington, D.C. 20434. Or you can phone the RTC Real Estate Information Center toll free at 1-800-431-0600. Be patient; the line most likely will be busy!

HUD Ads

Every Sunday, each "Real Estate for Sale" section of the classified ads of major newspapers, HUD (U.S. Department of Housing and Urban Development) runs a large ad. It lists the prices and addresses of homes foreclosed by the Veterans Administration (VA) and Federal Housing Administration (FHA).

Although you can get a good deal from this source, you have to be very careful. Why?

- HUD properties are sold only through real estate brokers. Therefore, they're listed at or close to market value.

- It's difficult to properly inspect HUD properties because all the utilities—gas, water, and electric—are usually turned off. Therefore, you may not know what works and what doesn't.

- Government red tape tests your patience.

- Financing by the government is not guaranteed. You may have to provide for your own through outside sources.

- The homes, sold "as is," pose a serious repair problem, because you don't really know what you're getting into, and the government will not offer any guarantees.

If you decide to try this source, I suggest you bid very low, complete all the proper prepurchase investigations, and hope for the best. In spite of all the difficulties, many patient people have gotten good buys from HUD.

IRS Tax Sales

Under the authority of sections 6331 and 6335 of the Internal Revenue Code, the U.S. government can seize a citizen's property—real and personal—as compensation for nonpayment of income taxes. The seized property is then auctioned off to the highest bidder at a tax sale. Besides real estate for sale, the IRS offers boats, cars, computer equipment, and just about anything else you can think of.

Although the IRS will "sell" for taxes due only, you must know that other liens—mortgages, property taxes, condominium association fees, state taxes, and so on—are not extinguished by an IRS sale. Many times, the accumulated total owed for all those liens exceeds the property's true market value. So do your homework and find out about the property.

IRS property is sold with no guarantees about the condition of the property. What you see is what you get.

There is a 180-day redemption period involved in the sale of any U.S. government-seized real estate. During that period, the former owner can reclaim the property. To do so, however, he or she must pay all the costs incurred by the successful bidder, plus a 20 percent yearly interest fee. At the end of an uncontested 180-day redemption period, the government will issue the new owner a deed. Up to that time, the only proof of ownership given was a certificate of sale.

When you attend an IRS auction, you'll have to have a cashier's check, a certified check, or a money order in a designated amount made payable to the IRS in order to bid.

To get in touch with IRS tax sales, call your local IRS office. Ask for the "seized property department." Tell the representative that you'd like to be placed on the IRS mailing list for real estate. Later, when you get a "Public Auction Sale" notice, it will list the following information:

- Date, time, and place of sale

- Title offered

- Property description

- Minimum bid

- Property inspection data

- Payment terms

- Form of payment

- Phone number to call for further information

- Other encumbrances on the property

- A warning that informs the prospective bidder to verify the validity, priority, and dollar amounts of any other encumbrances that may be due against the property

With the sources of hot buys I've given you here, you can select those that have the most appeal to you and work them out. When you do and you experience your first success, you'll agree with me that hard work and persistence pay off handsomely in real estate. It doesn't take a lot of money, a lofty position in society, or even luck, for that matter. I'm reminded of the old adage:

The harder I work, the luckier I get.

Scratching Up Your First Down Payment

It seems the amount of money you need for a down payment on your first real estate purchase continuously exceeds the amount of money you're able to save.

Without a windfall of cash either from an inheritance or the largesse of a friend or family member, odds are you'll never be able to reach your down payment objective. Now, that sounds downright pessimistic, doesn't it? But don't worry!

There are some unorthodox, creative financial arrangements available to you. They can provide your access to the world of real estate investing. But, I hasten to add, you must be willing to pour all your energy into uncovering them. The extent to which you're willing to use extra effort to discover and then employ unconventional financing techniques is equal to the intensity of your desire

51

to get into a real estate investment program. However, before I give you those optional arrangements, I have to mention the formidable challenge every investor from freshman to veteran has to face: Good credit.

As long as you structure a deal where you'll be relying on OPM— other people's money—you must have an acceptable credit history. Nobody will lend money to a poor credit risk.

Good credit is an incredibly powerful asset to have. Without it, your proposed investment career faces a formidable challenge; with it, the sky's the limit.

The first thing a lender does after receiving your loan application is to send to a credit reporting agency such as Trans Union for a credit report about you. When he receives the report, he'll carefully scrutinize it to assess your credit worthiness. If your report is riddled with numerous entries of late payments and other derogatory information, the lender will contact you and you'll have lots of explaining to do.

You should request a copy of the report and check it for its accuracy. You may find that some of the entries are wrong. If so, write a letter to each credit reporting agency—the major ones are listed in your phone directory—explaining the errors. The agency will communicate that information to the companies that reported the problems.

Each company has 30 days in which to respond. If the credit bureaus don't hear from them in that time period, the derogatory remarks will be deleted. If, on the other hand, the offended companies respond and claim the entries are accurate, they will remain in your report.

To be on the safe side, I recommend that you order your credit report yourself, before you apply for a loan. That way, you can clear up any negative entries before the document reaches your perspective lender. What a terrific impression you'd make if your report were clear—void of any negative entries! Remember, a strong credit report goes a long way toward getting loan approval.

Contacting the Big Three

How do you order your credit report? There are three major national credit reporting agencies: TRW Information Service, Equifax, and Trans Union. They're listed in the Yellow Pages of your phonebook. Equifax and Trans Union charge up to $15 for a credit report. However, as of May 1992, TRW Information Service will give one free report to anyone requesting it. All you have to do is write to

> TRW Consumer Assistance
> P.O. Box 2350
> Chatsworth, CA 91313-2350

To properly identify yourself, include the following information in your request:

> Full name
> Current address
> Previous address(es)
> Social security number
> Year of birth
> Spouse's name
> Photocopy of your driver's license
> Utility bill (to connect your name with your address)

Equifax, Trans Union, and TRW Information Service have recently responded to complaints from the federal government and the Consumer's Union in Washington, D.C. The complaints consisted of a "laundry list" of repeated consumer abuses perpetrated by the big three. It seems as though it was common company policy to trample on the rights of consumers.

Through the use of stiff fines and federal clout, the government persuaded the big three to institute these changes:

- Reduce the cost of credit reports to consumers.

- Furnish an easy-to-read report to the consumer within four days of his or her request.

- Furnish a free report if the consumer was denied a loan because of damaging credit information.

- Investigate and resolve, within 30 days, any entry disputed by the consumer, as outlined in the 1970 Fair Credit Reporting Act.

- Provide consumers with a corrected version of their credit reports after the resolution of disputes.

- If a consumer continues to disagree with a negative entry, permit the consumer to include a "dispute statement" in his or her report.

- Notify the consumer if a deleted item reappears on a subsequent report.

- Provide a toll-free number in order to respond to consumer inquiries. (As of the writing of this book, only Equifax has such a number: 1-800-685-1111).

You can obtain a merged report that combines credit information from TRW, Trans Union, and Equifax from the Credco service for $24 by writing

> Credco
> 2141 Palomar Airport Road
> Suite 200
> Carlsbad, CA 92009

Avoiding the "Credit Doctors"

They're out there! Learn to be careful and to avoid these charlatans. "Credit doctors" are people or firms that claim they can "cure" your credit problems by erasing any bad entries on your report. However, some of the schemes they use are clearly illegal.

For example, one company said that for a fee they would show their clients how to clean up their records by changing their social security numbers! Innocent victims would apply to the Internal Revenue Service for an employee identification number and then substitute that for their social security numbers. With the substitution, they'd create a different consumer, free of credit ills, a task made easier because both numbers contain nine digits.

Any change or alteration to a social security number is against the law, and lenders automatically deny people loans who have tried to alter their numbers.

Credit Maintenance

Generally, people with credit problems are the victims of their own poor judgment. Everyone should cultivate good credit as a matter of course and not wait until a loan application brings it to his or her attention.

Establish the habit of paying statements from department stores, banks, and S&Ls immediately. If you can't do it that quickly, as a reminder, write the payment's due date on the envelope and make sure your remittance is mailed to arrive before the deadline noted.

Preventive Maintenance

If you have a crisis that temporarily makes it impossible for you to make your monthly payments, contact your creditors. Explain your situation to them. Ask them for extensions of your loans and a reduction in your minimum monthly payments.

At the same time, restructure your budget to cut expenses wherever possible. If you have difficulty doing that, call the local office of the Consumer Credit Counseling Service (CCCS). That national nonprofit organization may be able to help you. It's listed in your phone directory. At your request, a CCCS representative will contact your creditors and set up a new, extended payment schedule. Each month you'll make a single payment to the CCCS, which will parcel out payments to your creditors. For that service, CCCS charges a small monthly fee.

Cosigner

If you have an excessive number of unexcused derogatory payment entries; if your former property was foreclosed on; if you have outstanding judgments; if you've gone bankrupt; or if you have any write-offs—meaning your creditors have given up on you—your credit status poses a special problem. Notice I said "special problem"—not necessarily a roadblock.

Lenders consider a poor credit history to be a "character" flaw. "Character," along with "capacity" and "collateral," are the major criteria on which a lender bases his or her appraisal of you as a potential borrower.

In order to boost the lender's assessment of you, you're going to have to find someone with a sound credit status to vouch for you. You'll need a *cosigner*, someone with a strong credit history whom the lender will rely on to make payments in the event you fail to do so. A cosigner could be your financial savior.

Money lenders request cosigners for applicants with no credit history at all. To avoid being in that situation, establish a credit history as soon as possible.

An easy way to create a sound credit rating is to open a checking or savings account. After you've become a reliable depositor, your bank or S&L will offer you a credit card. You should accept the offer but use the card very judiciously. Each month go out and buy a necessary something on credit. Then, as soon as you get billed from the lender, promptly submit a payment. You'll be doing two important things: You'll be establishing a good credit history and, by paying promptly, you'll be saving the cost of interest. The notoriously high credit card interest begins to accrue after the lapse of the posted payment due date on the bill.

The first and most obvious people to turn to when you need a cosigner are your parents. If such a move is not feasible, try some other close family member, or possibly a trusting friend. If you have no relative or friend to turn to—or if you're too embarrassed to ask—you can run an ad in the paper asking for help. There are people who, for a one-time fee, will agree to lend their credit power to you. The fee is usually 5 percent of the loan amount up to $1 million. Beyond that sum, the rate declines. Remember, the fee is to be paid after the loan is ready for funding, not before.

Instead of a fee, you can try offering the cosigner a piece of the action. If you're buying a property to fix and sell, he or she may accept a percentage of the profits. Or, if you intend to keep the property as a rental, you can offer the cosigner a percentage of ownership. Make sure all your terms are in writing in a contract prepared by a knowledgeable attorney.

Be careful of scams. Some fraudulent cosigners attempt to collect all or a portion of their fee up front. After they receive that money, those sleuths disappear and leave their innocent, credit-poor victims high and dry.

A legitimate cosigner could be your ticket to the world of real estate investing. Don't let poor credit be a barricade to your success. Don't let anything stop you! If you need a cosigner at all, it'll probably be for your first deal only. Then, after you've become a reliable borrower, you may be asked to be a cosigner yourself.

Credit Cards as Sources of Capital

In the world of credit card lenders, more is better! That's right. The more credit cards you have, the higher is your credit esteem among them. Some credit card companies set very minimal requirements for card acquisitions. Take advantage of that and apply for as many as you can. Your possession of numerous cards can make a substantial sum of money available to you for a down payment on property.

The exorbitant interest rates charged make "plastic money" loans the most expensive in the financial marketplace. However, they're acceptable for fast-turnaround projects—buy, fix, sell.

As long as you're disciplined and pay them off immediately after your sale, credit card loans are a legitimate alternative method to finance your first real estate transaction.

Getting $100,000 Cash with Credit Cards

People can obtain more than $100,000 in cash advances with credit cards—all legal transactions. Do you wonder how it's possible?

It's an easy but fairly expensive way to go. Mastercard, Visa, and other plastic merchants offer takeout cash in amounts up to your credit line's limit. Usually, you simply go to a bank, show your card, sign your name, and walk out with money—no questions asked.

Know that the interest rates are high—anywhere from 10 to 20 percent! But that's the price you pay for a rather effortless way to get a bank loan with none of the bank's collateral requirements, income and savings verification, and no other form of security.

Also, on premium or "gold" cards, your credit line usually starts anywhere from $5,000 and up. With just 10 cards, you could obtain up to $50,000 for your investments.

As you go off in search of multiple cards, keep in mind that each issuing bank orders a credit report on you. As a first step in the process, order your own credit report, clear up any uncomplimentary entires, and *then* make multiple credit card applications.

Inquiries

An inquiry is an entry that's made on your credit report yet does not of itself affect your creditworthiness. All credit applicants have inquiries on their credit reports. They're added every time you apply for credit and contain the name of the company investigating you and the date of inquiry.

The more credit you seek, the more inquiries are added to your report. Lenders, being fiscally conservative, don't like viewing too many inquiries in their borrowers' reports. These banking officers become skeptical of you and may deny you a prospective loan.

Inquiries remain on your credit report for nine months to a year. The problem? How do you force multiple inquiries to be eradicated? Try the following approaches:

- Write a letter to the credit reporting agencies, asking them to remove their inquiries from your file. You can give as a reason the fact that you've been denied credit because the inquiries are on file. Offer to pay the clerical expenses incurred.

• Write a letter to the credit reporting agencies, explaining that you don't recall applying for credit with the companies listed.

When you apply for several credit cards, attempt to keep some of your multiple inquiries hidden from your selected lenders by submitting all your applications simultaneously.

Signature Loans and Lines of Credit

An investor's heaven-on-earth could be something like this: Walk into a bank, sign a loan document of some kind, and later walk out with money. Imagine, nothing collateralized, nothing pledged—only a signature on a formalized IOU.

Would you believe that such a heaven-on-earth scenario exists? Well, it does. It's called a *signature loan* or an *unsecured line of credit*. I've personally used that outlet to raise capital many times. It's another wonderful financing alternative, and it earned me hundreds of thousands of dollars in profits over the years I've been in business.

"Where do you get such loans?" you eagerly ask. Well, not all commercial lenders make them. On the other hand, there are lenders out there who specialize in that type of business.

"How do you locate them?" Simple. You "walk through" the Yellow Pages of your phone book—just as I did. Start at the beginning of the listings for banks. Call each one until you unearth the institution that can accommodate you.

After you've located your lender-benefactor, you'll have to qualify for the loan. You must be able to show the lender that you enjoy job stability, have a current income with enough excess cash to make the monthly payment on the proposed loan, and possess a clean credit history.

The interest rate on a signature loan is usually tied to the prime rate—the rate banks charge their best business customers. Of course, you pay interest only on the funds actually withdrawn. The payback period is of short duration—six months to a year, in my experience. But that's long enough to do a "flip" project (a quick-buy-and-fix-up deal, also known as a fast-turnaround project), which, incidentally, is another very neat way to finance that kind of a deal.

One caveat: Pay your lender on time. Don't ask the lender for an extension. That will make him or her very nervous, and maybe the next time you want a signature loan you'll be turned down. Lenders are your best silent partners. Treat them with respect and kindness.

Even when I'm flush with cash, I prefer to fund an entire project with borrowed money. It's great to begin a deal with 100 percent borrowed funds, sell the property, pay off the lenders, and deposit the profits. It's about as close to creating something from nothing that I'll ever get!

As with credit cards, it's possible to get many signature loans—all at the same time. Remember: The more money you borrow, the more money you can make.

By managing the repayment of several loans, you're forced to learn the proper care and handling of money. You're also forced to make a personal commitment to succeed. Leverage creates wealth. Locate the lender that can help you.

Remember, different lenders specialize in different kinds of loans. For example, I had an interesting experience trying to locate a lender who would use some of my first *trust deeds* that I owned as collateral for a loan. I needed the money for a conversion project I was working on. A *trust deed* is a legal document that conveys title to property to a third party until the borrower pays off the loan.

I started by asking for loans at all of the traditional institutions, including those with whom I had had many years of affiliation. They all turned me down. They explained that they could lend on real property, machinery, vehicles, or inventory but not on trust deeds.

So, after I exhausted the list of traditional lenders, I started to call alternative lenders—finance companies, for instance. To my surprise, they were not only willing but even eager to make me the loan.

Do you see my point? You have to have a dogged determination to seek out what you're looking for. Don't give up. And never take a "no" from one or a dozen lenders to be the final answer to your problem. Keep looking. Your "yes" could be the next listing down!

Institutional Shylocks

Always ready to prey on the misfortunes of others, certain lenders look for and cater to people with serious credit problems. These potential borrowers have been rejected by traditional banks and S&Ls.

Maybe not in the strict Shakespearean sense, they're nonetheless "institutional Shylocks." They advertise grandiose claims that they'll make you a loan even if you've had a foreclosure, a judgment, and write-offs. And, they probably will. What they don't advertise is what it's going to cost. And, it costs dearly. Those lenders usually

- Charge outrageous loan fees

- Charge higher interest rates

- Restrict the term of the loan to only a few years, leaving you with a huge balloon payment (total payback in one huge payment) looming on the horizon

- Offer a loan to value ratio of only 65 percent for a first trust deed but will write a concurrent second as well

- Set the stage for you to default so that they can foreclose and take over the property

Be sure you don't fall prey to these ripoff artists. Use only safe, legitimate alternative financing. Avoid the Shylocks like the plague. By intelligently seeking out the right lenders, you can forge financial plans that will be safe and ultimately rewarding.

Tips for Completing Your Loan Application

Sometimes credit applicants become their own worst enemy. They fail to portray themselves in the most favorable light. Essentially, they understate income and overstate debt. That contributes to the fact that the majority of loan applications are turned down.

To increase your odds of becoming one of the minority whose applications are approved, follow these tips:

- Include all the complimentary personal data you can accumulate.

- Divulge uncomplimentary information only if it is specially requested.

- Word process or type your application.

- Connect an answering machine to the phone line you list on the application or get an answering service to ensure you don't miss calls from the lender.

- List only dependents whom you truly support.

- Ensure that you have a savings or checking account in your name at a local bank.

- List credit references only if your accounts show up on your credit report. It's unnecessary to reveal that you owe a relative money, for example.

- Make your income as substantial and your job title as impressive as possible.

- Show the occupancy at your current address to be as long as possible.

Now you're ready to submit your application to your lender. However,

---

Submit the loan application to a lender only if the loan officer gives it a good chance of being approved.

Otherwise, you'll just rack up another meddlesome inquiry in your credit file!

Seller-Assisted Financing

Suppose the ideas of using credit cards, signature loans, and cosigners as sources of capital don't appeal to you. Well, here's another alternative. This one involves the seller. Read on.

As you search for down payment money, don't overlook the sellers. Sellers often don't advertise the fact that they'll "carry back" a second trust deed.

In carrying back a second trust deed, the sellers in effect lend you some equity in the property for a stated length of time. The sellers' security for doing so will be a lien placed on the property via a trust deed. To give public notice of the sellers' continuing interest in the property, they record the trust deed in the county where the property is located. Because this trust deed is recorded subsequent to the date on which the first trust deed was recorded, this new document is the "second" trust deed.

In lending you some of their equity in the property, sellers reduce the amount of money you need for a down payment.

Sellers don't usually advertise that they'll accept something other than cash as a down payment. But you don't know what a seller *will* accept until you make an offer. Not all sellers are locked into receiving all cash for the sale. Be creative!

If the sellers own the property free and clear and are willing to carry back a first trust deed or have an assumable first trust deed with a cooperative lender, try the following:

- Ask your sellers to carry back a second trust deed for the difference between their assumable first trust deed and your purchase price. The second deed offers tax advantages for the seller. Rather than pay the IRS a large lump sum for their profit, they'll pay smaller increments yearly over the term of the second mortgage. Sweeten the deal by offering a higher-than-usual interest rate for the loan, a price a few thousand over market, and give the sellers postdated checks for the first 12 payments.

- Ask your sellers to accept assets other than cash as a down payment. Suppose you're a buyer with a lot of "toys"—a motor boat, a sailboat, a motorhome, a vintage car—you know what I mean. Ask the sellers to accept one or more of your "toys" as a down payment. Maybe between a combination of your "toys" and a second trust deed, you can strike a no-cash deal. Truth is, you don't know until you ask.

- Ask the sellers to accept the down payment in installments. If they want $20,000 as the down payment, offer $2,000 at the close of escrow with a written promise to pay the remainder in increments of $2,000 plus interest every three months for 27 months. You can sweeten the deal by paying a slightly higher price for the property or a slightly higher rate than the going percentage of interest. You can even give the sellers postdated checks for the first two ensuing payments.

Chapter 5 contains more ideas for seller-assisted purchases.

Two Legitimate Ways to Reduce Down Payments

Broker's Fee as a Trust Deed

A little preplanning can reduce your down payment's cash outlay considerably while you still satisfy the seller's need for proceeds from the sale.

Many real estate deals involve a broker—and a broker's fees. I propose to have the broker take the commission in the form of a junior trust deed in order to reduce the cash needed to make the purchase. You can make this setup a condition of the sale.

For instance, say the purchase price of a piece of real estate is $200,000 and the seller is insisting on $20,000 down. If the sale is consummated, the seller will receive $200,000 less the broker's fee of $12,000 (6 percent of $200,000), for a net of $188,000. That's before escrow charges and paying off the existing trust deed that has a $100,000 balance, of course.

If the broker were to take the commission in the form of a second trust deed against the property, the seller would have the cash expenses of sale outlay reduced by $12,000. The necessity to pay the broker's commission in cash would be eliminated. The buyer would then be able to purchase the property with a down payment of only $8,000.

To satisfy the lender, you may have to make this sort of adjustment during escrow, after loan approval.

It may not be easy to talk a broker into accepting this kind of deal. However, you should negotiate at the onset of your contact with the broker to make this setup a contingency of the sale.

I'm a broker, and I've accepted second trust deeds instead of cash to finalize some deals. I did it reluctantly—but I did it. I believe in the old saying that "A bird in hand is worth two in the bush." Today it's not that unusual for brokers to assist buyers by accepting a trust deed in lieu of a cash commission at closing.

The real problem with this kind of deal lies with the broker's agency. But the job of convincing the agency to go along with you rests with your broker, not you.

One advantage of the broker's acceptance of a second trust deed in lieu of cash commission is the tax benefit of receiving incremental payments versus a lump sum commission. Instead of one large tax payment on the commission, taxes are due only as the smaller payments are received.

If you're purchasing the property to do a flip deal, your broker probably will not object to accepting a trust deed, because you can shorten the term of the deed to a year or less. This setup is especially appealing to the broker if you agree to give that broker the listing to sell the rehabbed property.

To contrast the traditional commission scenario with the reduced-cash illustration, look at the following sample deal that shows the same transaction with cash to the broker and then with a trust deed to the broker. In both cases, the property sells for the same price, and the seller nets the same; but in the second financing setup, the buyer can come into the deal with $12,000 less cash.

Case 1. Cash to Broker Scenario for $200,000 Sale

Seller's Proceeds:

$	20,000	Buyer's down payment
	180,000	Payment from buyer's trust deed
−	12,000	Real estate commission
−	100,000	Balance on seller's trust deed
$	88,000	Net cash to seller

Buyer's Cash Outlay:

$	200,000	Sale price of property
−	180,000	Buyer's trust deed to pay seller
$	20,000	Cash needed by buyer for down payment

Case 2. Trust Deed to Broker Scenario for $200,000 Sale

Seller's Proceeds:

$	8,000	Buyer's down payment
	180,000	Payment from buyer's trust deed
−	100,000	Balance on seller's trust deed
$	88,000	Net cash to seller

Buyer's Cash Outlay:

$	200,000	Sale price of property
−	180,000	Buyer's first trust deed to pay seller
−	12,000	Buyer's second trust deed to pay broker
$	8,000	Cash needed by buyer for down payment

Cash needed by buyer: $8,000

The buyer would then own the property with a first trust deed of $180,000, and a second trust deed payable to the broker for $12,000.

Timing Your Closing to Obtain the Rents

If you purchase an apartment house, you can reduce your down payment by properly timing the close of escrow to the date the rents are due. Let me show you how this works.

First of all, remember that rents are paid in advance. Suppose the total monthly rents on a 10-unit building you're buying amount to $5,000, and they are due on the first of the month. Try to time the closing of your escrow to that precise date. As the new owner of the building, those rents will belong to you. A simple instruction to your escrow officer to credit you with the rents due will automatically give you a $5,000 reduction in the cash you need for your down payment.

If you also include the tenants' last month rents, and their security deposits, you can reduce your down payment requirement even further, as shown here.

Reducing Cash to Purchase a $300,000 Apartment House

$	50,000	Down payment required
5,000		Rents due on the first of the month
5,000		Last month's rent on deposit
2,500		Security deposits credited to buyer
–	12,500	Total credits to buyer
$	37,500	Net cash needed for down payment

Now, if there's a broker involved—and there usually is in an apartment house deal—have the real estate agency take the 6 percent commission in the form of a trust deed, as just explained. That way, you can generate another cash reduction:

$	37,500	Net cash needed after credit for rents due, last month's rents, and security deposits
–	18,000	Less real estate agent's commission of 6% of $300,000
$	19,500	Cash needed for down payment

The buyer would sign a note and trust deed to the broker for $18,000, using the apartment house as security.

Locating money for your first down payment is a formidable task but not an impossible one. It's a wonderful, rewarding challenge. With patience, perseverance, and positive thinking, you can and will find that perfect solution.

In 1981 I decided I was young enough to retire. With a huge, beautiful home and a substantial yearly income from my trust deeds, my multimillionaire status was firmly established. I felt it was time for me to taste the good life.

Well, I retired for about eight months. The idea of playing golf and puttering around the garden got a little boring. I felt I was wasting my time. So, guess what? I unretired. I decided to get back into real estate.

Not wanting to touch my retirement income or savings, I decided to challenge myself again and try starting over using none of my own capital. Needless to say, I used some of the ideas I've given you in this chapter and again proceeded to amass more wealth for myself and family.

My interest in retirement has not been rekindled. I'm still in this wonderful business and love every minute of it.

CHAPTER 5

Nothing Down:
Myths and Realities

Through the pages of a national best seller and the hawking of late-night television real estate experts, the term "no down payment" has been spread across America.

Masses of people from all walks of life spent tens of millions of hard-earned dollars on books and tapes, all purporting to unlock the secrets to acquiring property with no down payment—or so the authors claimed.

Well, as time passed, it turned out that most of those no-down authors went bankrupt. They were put there by the very customers who purchased the authors' books and tapes, then later returned that merchandise, demanding their money back.

People found that although they made fascinating reading and listening, the authors' carefully orchestrated no-down deals were too difficult to emulate in the real world. Why? Because they omitted some very important details such as these:

- Where does the money come from to pay the buyer's escrow and finance fees?

- How do you pay a broker's commission when sources of cash, such as down payment and refinance, may be absent from the deal?

71

- How do you buy with nothing down and still negotiate a discount price?

- How do you handle the setbacks faced by the buyer and the risks of the seller when you purchase with nothing down?

- What are the exact escrow instructions used to effect a no-down deal?

- How can you buy with no money down and yet get new conventional financing or assume a non-VA loan?

Those unanswered questions left the student-investor out on a limb when he or she tried to do a no-down deal. It also seriously eroded the readers' confidence in those authors' authority.

As I understand it, the term "no down payment" has four quite different meanings:

- No actual cash is invested by the buyer; he or she buys the property with 100 percent financing.

- The down payment will consist not of cash but of something such as an IOU, a trust deed, or another tangible asset.

- The down payment is borrowed from a friend or family member and does not come from the pocket of the buyer.

- The buyer borrows the down payment through the use of a signature loan, equity loan, or credit card.

It would be easier to make a no-down purchase if you found

- An owner desperate to sell in a buyer's market

- An owner willing to carry back a first or second trust deed

- An owner unaware of the risks he or she may incur

- An owner willing to engage in secret negotiations outside of escrow contrived to fool the lender into thinking that the buyer made a down payment when in fact there was none (necessary only if the deal required the buyer to assume an existing non-VA loan or apply for a new conventional one)

Buyer's Setbacks in a No-Down Deal

Just in case you're not yet convinced that there is no free lunch in purchasing distressed properties, explore the ways you would pay more than you saved if you tried making a no-down deal.

Excessive Price

For the buyer, there are a couple of aspects of buying property with nothing down that may detract somewhat from its general allure—especially when the point is to buy distressed property inexpensively. The first—and to me, the most important—is price.

Unless a buyer is an award winning negotiator, he or she will not get a distressed investment house from a private party at least 15 percent under market *and at the same time* purchase it with no down payment. That's just not going to happen in the real world. It's unrealistic to expect *both* best terms—no down payment and a price 15 percent under market.

Instead of buying at a discount, the buyer may very well end up paying a price for the property that exceeds its true market value. So the immediate saving of skipping a down payment may reduce the profit earned from the total net return later.

Negative Cash Flow

Remember this: An investment property purchased with no down payment—a property 100 percent leveraged—will *not* generate enough monthly rental income to cover loan payments, taxes, insurance, and other expenses. Anyone who disputes that is either not being honest or has never owned investment property.

The difference between the monthly income and monthly expenses will have to come from somewhere. But where? Well, if the investor has a savings account, funds will have to come from there as needed to cover the monthly income shortage. If an investor has residual income from his or her salary, that source is of course available. But, in any event, whether the buyer puts his or her money into a down payment up front or uses it a little at a time monthly, the investor is going to have to ultimately use cash to carry the property.

My philosophy has always been to try to buy the property substantially under market. That's the first priority. With that done, I will have already made money on the deal.

Later, the addition of value through appreciation will ultimately amount to a windfall profit. When the property appreciates to a point where I could refinance and take out all my money—down payment, fix-up expenses, and holding costs—I'd do so. The belated recapture of my cash invested could be called a "delayed no-down" deal.

An Examination of Some No-Down and "Cash After Purchase" Deals

This section describes some no-down and "cash after purchase" transactions that are familiar to me. I find them fascinating, but they do contain elements of risk for the seller and buyer. If you decide to try to use them, proceed carefully, with your eyes wide open. Seek legal advice whenever you have a doubt or a problem.

- Seller takes back a first trust deed for the entire sale price of his or her free-and-clear property.

- Seller agrees to subordination.

- Seller agrees to substitution of collateral.

- Seller accepts as down payment something other than cash.

- Seller accepts an offer in excess of the asking price, then shares the new loan proceeds with the buyer.

- Seller accepts 100 percent leverage.

- Seller accepts zero coupon bonds.

Now, let's go into details of each of these procedures.

Seller Takes Back a First Trust Deed

In this case, the seller takes back a first trust deed for the entire sale price of his or her free-and-clear property. The buyer would have no cash invested at all. Because the buyer has nothing at risk, he could

- Accumulate mechanic's liens

- Incur an IRS lien

- Run down the property

- Accumulate unpaid property taxes

- Stop making loan payments to the seller

- Force a foreclosure action

The seller could eventually take over the property but he in the meantime would have lost the income from the note. Additionally, the seller would reassume the property subject to the previous owner's liens. Finally, very likely, the seller would have to rehab the place in order to resell it.

However, this is a great deal for an honorable investor, one who can use this technique to gain an entrance into the real estate market.

Consider yourself extremely lucky to find an owner of free-and-clear property who will sell the property to you with no down payment.

Anytime a seller takes back a note, instead of receiving cash, he or she gets a tax break. How? Well, by receiving the profits a little at a time via monthly payments, the seller avoids paying a large one-time tax on the profit from the sale. It's a good idea to use this fact as an inducement for the seller to carry back the trust deed for you.

Subordination

If the seller is unaware of the implications of the word *subordination* as used in real estate trust deeds, the seller can easily have his or her security interest in a property compromised or even completely wiped out.

It can happen like this: The seller owns the property free and clear. The buyer convinces the seller to carry back a first trust deed for the entire purchase price. Somewhere in the fine print of the note is a statement that reads:

> Holder of this note agrees to subordination.

That means that the seller, who holds the first trust deed, agrees to go into a *junior position* if the buyer decides to refinance the property. An unscrupulous buyer could get new financing in an amount that could wipe out the equity supporting the seller's note.

This is a "cash after purchase" deal that gives the buyer the opportunity to extract money from the property without having anything invested in it.

If there were a broker involved in this sort of transaction, it probably wouldn't work. Why? Because the normal sources used to pay a commission—cash from down payment or refinancing—are absent from the transaction.

Substitution of Collateral

Say that, as part of the buyer's offer, the seller agrees to take back a trust deed for all or a portion of the sale price. On top of that, the buyer talks the seller into giving him or her the right to remove the subject property as the security for the note and to replace it with other property the buyer may own (called the *substitution of collateral*).

This is not too beneficial for the seller unless there's sufficient equity in the substitute property to protect the amount of the seller's trust deed. It should be the buyer's responsibility to provide the seller with all the documentation necessary to guarantee the safety of the seller's interest.

This is another opportunity for a shrewd buyer to extract cash from the property after purchasing it. How? Well, by removing the subject property as security for the seller's note, the buyer may then generate some cash by going out and getting a new loan against it.

Three "Something Other Than Cash as Down Payment" Plans

Another alternative to no-down and cash after purchase deals are described in the three types of plans outlined here.

Plan 1. Seller Accepts the Buyer's IOU

If the seller, in place of cash, accepts the buyer's promissory note—an IOU—as the down payment, it's great for the buyer. But if the buyer turns out to be dishonest, the seller will be faced with double jeopardy.

Because the promissory note is merely the buyer's "promise" to pay, the seller has little recourse if the buyer defaults. Sure, the seller can go to court and obtain a judgment, but that's costly and may prove futile if the buyer has no assets and no job. Very likely, the seller will end up with a worthless piece of paper.

Remember, the seller can't foreclose, because his or her property was not used as the collateral for the promissory note.

Conclusion:

The IOU, accepted as a down payment instrument, is risky business for the seller but a great idea for an honest buyer.

Plan 2. Seller Accepts the Buyer's Junior Trust Deed

In this no-down scenario, the seller is asked to accept as down payment a second or third trust deed that the buyer owns. That may be okay, as long as the seller takes the time to thoroughly investigate the property used as the collateral for the buyer's note. A seller should find out how many notes are in front of the one offered, along with the market value of the property. From that information, the seller can determine whether there's enough equity to support the note.

It would be unwise for the seller to accept the buyer's junior trust deed if the property it encumbers is burdened with loans that total more than 50 percent of its market value.

In this situation, the seller should make the buyer pay for a complete title search to disclose all the recorded liens on the property, along with any unpaid real estate taxes.

Plan 3. Seller's Second Trust Deed As a Substitute Down Payment

The third "something other than cash" down payment deal works as follows: The buyer asks the seller to take back a second trust deed for the difference between the sales price and the assumable first trust deed. The seller's second trust deed is the buyer's "substitute" cashless down payment.

The problem here is that because the buyer has no cash invested, he or she can easily walk away from the property without any personal loss. After possibly incurring mechanic's and IRS liens, along with amassing unpaid property taxes, the buyer could stop making payments on the seller's note. The seller, forced to foreclose, could find out that his or her equity had been seriously eroded by the other property liens incurred by the errant buyer.

Cash to Buyer:
An Offer in Excess of Asking Price

In this scheme, the buyer offers to purchase the property for a figure that exceeds the asking price. The elated seller is then asked to refinance the property with a new assumable first trust deed in an amount equal to about 75 percent of the property's appraised value.

The buyer could then make a case that says because he or she is paying more than the asking price for the property, the buyer should share in the funds generated by the refinancing. With the buyer's portion of those funds, he or she promises to make improvements on the property.

As a final condition of purchase, the buyer requests the seller to take back as a second trust deed, the difference between the purchase price and the new first trust deed. Let's see how this looks:

Status of the Property Before the Sale

$	150,000	Original asking price
–	75,000	Existing first mortgage
$	75,000	Seller's equity before costs of sale

Status of the Property at the Acceptance of the Buyer's Offer

$	180,000	Sale price offered by buyer
–	75,000	Existing first mortgage
$	105,000	Seller's inflated equity

79

Status of the Property After Refinancing and Sale

$	180,000	Sale price
−	112,500	New first trust deed at 75% of bank appraisal of $150,000
+	67,500	Seller's second trust deed
$	180,000	Total encumbrances

Cash Generated After Refinance and Sale

$	112,500	New first trust deed
−	13,500	Points, loan escrow and 6% real estate commission
	99,000	Net proceeds from refinancing before paying off old note
−	75,000	Pay off old note
	24,000	Net cash from refinancing
−	12,000	Cash to buyer
$	12,000	Cash to seller

Seller's Position After Refinancing and Sale

$	180,000	Inflated sale price
−	112,500	New first trust deed
+	67,500	Seller's second trust deed
+	12,000	Cash received from refinancing
$	79,500	Total received after sale

Buyer's Position After Refinancing and Sale

$	180,000	Sale price
−	112,500	First trust deed
−	67,500	Second trust deed
+	12,000	Cash received from seller's refinance
$	0	Cash invested

The buyer now owns a property appraised by the bank at $150,000 with $180,000 worth of liens! This is a case where some fancy footwork would have to be done to fool the lender into thinking that a down payment was made. Why? Because conventional lenders do not permit the assumption of their loans without the buyer proving that he or she made a substantial down payment on the property!

Because the property is encumbered for more than its bank appraisal, the face value of the seller's second trust deed is eroded by about 50 percent.

The buyer has no cash invested, and on top of that, *received* cash from the refinancing; therefore, the buyer really has no stake in the property, a property appraised at $150,000 and encumbered with $180,000 worth of loans. Result? Foreclosure, most likely.

The seller will have to repossess the property. But then the seller will inherit a loan of $112,500 instead of $75,000, and the former $75,000 gross equity will have been reduced to $37,500! In all probability, the buyer will have accumulated some past-due payments on the first trust deed and any number of other liens—all of them now becoming the responsibility of the seller.

One Hundred Percent Leverage

Here's another no-down scheme you'll find interesting:

1. The buyer asks the seller to take out a second trust deed on the property—at the seller's expense. The seller agrees.

2. The second trust deed lender will come out, appraise the property, and allow a second trust deed loan in an amount equal to the difference between the existing first trust deed and 75 percent of the property's appraised value. The seller's loan proceeds from the second trust deed are supposed to take the place of the buyer's down payment.

3. It's the buyer's intention to assume both the first and second trust deeds. In order to do that, the buyer and the seller will have to engage in some sort of secret documentation outside of escrow designed to fool the lender into thinking that a down payment was made.

4. Through the use of subterfuge, let's assume the buyer was able to take over both trust deeds. Then, the buyer will ask the seller to carry back a third trust deed for the difference between the sale price and the total of the first and second trust deeds.

5. Result: The buyer bought the property with no down payment; but it's encumbered by three trust deeds in an aggregate amount equal to the purchase price.

6. What does the seller have? The seller winds up with the proceeds from the second trust deed, less the lender's points and broker's fees, and a third trust deed on the property. This time, the seller traded an orchard for an apple! The seller allowed a buyer to take possession of the property without a dime of his or her own money invested in it. All the seller has from the deal are the net proceeds from the second trust deed and the seller's own third trust deed.

If the buyer walks away—which is certainly possible if he or she suffers a job loss or some other financial setback—the buyer would incur no personal loss.

In the event foreclosure comes about, the seller will repossess the property, now encumbered with two loans rather than one, and have the entire sale process to go through all over again.

Zero Coupon Bonds

Here's another incredibly creative purchase plan involving zero coupon bonds, bonds bought at a discount price whose interest accrues to the face value to the date of maturity.

Rather than providing for the payment of interest monthly or quarterly as is the usual case for investment bonds, zero coupon bonds do something different. The interest on zero coupon bonds accumulates to the date of maturity, at which time it is paid out in one lump sum. However, for federal income tax purposes, the owners of the bonds must report the interest earned yearly, even though they haven't received it.

Zero coupon bonds have various maturity dates, but for real estate purposes, those coming due in 20 years appear to be the most popular. You can purchase them for a price that's just a fraction of their face value at maturity.

I became intimately aware of zero coupon bonds when a buyer made me a full-price offer of $130,000 for a condo I owned free and clear. Here was his proposal:

- Purchase price, $130,000, with $30,000 down.

- For the $100,000 balance of my equity, he offered me $350,000 worth of zero coupon bonds due in 20 years (that meant that after 20 years, I would cash in the bonds for $350,000).

On the surface, it sounded pretty good to me, I have to admit. Then I stepped back and analyzed the situation. Here's what I found out the buyer was up to:

1. After opening escrow, the buyer was to go to a lender and apply for a loan for $80,000. That loan would have been relatively easy to get because $80,000 was only about 60 percent of the value of the condo.

2. With the $80,000 proceeds of the loan, the buyer would use $30,000 to cover his down payment, and $50,000 to purchase the $350,000 worth of zero coupon bonds.

3. The buyer would take over the $130,000 condo with an $80,000 loan and an immediate $50,000 equity.

4. I, the seller, was to receive $30,000 cash and $350,000 worth of 20-year zero coupon bonds at the close of escrow.

5. The buyer wanted me to give him the right to assign his offer to a third party. That meant that while making an $80,000 deal with me, he would be looking for a $130,000 buyer for himself. If he were successful, he'd pick up an immediate $50,000 profit—without investing a dime! (Do you wonder how people think up these deals?)

Of course, after understanding his proposed deal, I turned him down. I figured that if I wanted $350,000 worth of 20-year zero coupon bonds and $30,000 cash, I could get my own $80,000 loan against the condo.

In investigating the purchase of zero coupon bonds, I discovered that some investment institutions that sold them would lend you 90 percent of their present value and then take them back as security. So, that meant that I could spend $50,000 on $350,000 worth of bonds, and get $45,000 (90 percent of $50,000) cash back in the form of a loan. The result? I'd have an $80,000 loan against the condo, a $45,000 loan against the bonds, $75,000 cash ($30,000 plus $45,000), $350,000 worth of pledged zero coupon bonds, and still own the $130,000 condo with an equity of $50,000 in it.

I hope it's clear to you why I turned the offer down! But it was a very creative idea.

Buying property with as little personal cash as possible is every real estate investor's goal. To use as much OPM (other people's money) as safely possible is never a bad idea, as long as you have honorable intentions.

Investors, generally speaking, are not unscrupulous or dishonest. Therefore, no-down transactions can be accomplished honorably. The interests of the seller can be secure. At the same time, the buyer can take advantage of entering the wonderful world of real estate without the necessity of having lots of cash. Remember, these creative financing deals can only happen here in America!

Is this a great country, or what?

How to Get the Loan You Need

Determining how much financing you need is vital to the distressed real estate investment process. To accurately estimate the loan you need, you first need to decide whether you'll occupy the property you're about to purchase.

You must decide about occupancy *before* you seek financing. All lenders finance owner-occupied property deals, but many don't finance nonowner-occupied exchanges. Occupancy is thus an important issue with lenders. If you obtain a loan on the condition that you'll occupy the property and then don't do so, the lender can call in the loan.

Finding a lender for nonowner-occupied property is usually not a problem. You can expect to pay slightly higher points for the loan and a slightly higher interest rate. Simply scan the phonebook listings for lenders that advertise cooperation on such deals.

Your decision about occupying the property involves another factor: the size of the loan. For an owner-occupied distressed property, a conventional lender will lend up to 90 percent of the property's appraised value, but for a nonowner-occupied property the lender will loan just 80 percent of the property's appraised value. Also, FHA and VA financing (described in Chapter 7) currently is unavailable for nonowner-occupied properties.

If you decide not to occupy the property as you rehab it and still want to make just a 10 percent down payment, you can turn to the sellers for further negotiations about a second trust deed, as described in Chapter 5. If a seller-backed trust deed doesn't work out, check the phonebook again for lenders that advertise a specialty in secondary financing. Their fees and interest rates may be high, but for short-term flip deals you shouldn't count this source out.

Be upright and honest in your dealings with lenders. They are your key to financial success. Use as much of their money as possible, then make paying them back your first priority.

It may not appear that way when you apply, but the last thing a lender wants to do is deny you a loan. Lending institutions gauge their success by the amount of current, outstanding loans they have on their books. To a borrower, a loan is a liability; to a lender, it's an asset.

Although lenders want and need your business, they must favorably assess you in three critical areas in order to approve your loan.

"So what are those three critical areas?" you ask.

Capacity, Collateral, and Character

To get a lender to approve your loan request, you must give him or her encouraging, positive signals about your "capacity" to repay the loan; your "collateral" to secure the loan; and your general "character," primarily, your creditworthiness.

Capacity

If you intend to live in the distressed property, to meet the capacity requirement, you must show the lender that you have sufficient income to meet your proposed monthly loan payment. Although it varies among different lenders, most of them figure that a home loan payment of principal, interest, real estate taxes, and insurance (a foursome abbreviated as PITI) should not exceed 30 to 33 percent of you and your spouse's combined monthly net income.

However, suppose you decide not to move into your distressed property and treat the purchase as a pure investment. By doing so you add another element to your "capacity" qualification: You'll have rental income. Even if you intend to do a flip deal, the lender, in judging your capacity, will treat your deal as if you were purchasing the property for rental purposes only.

In processing your loan, the lender will ask what you believe the monthly income from the property will be. The loan officer will also check the projected income estimate with local real estate agents. Say the consensus is that the property should bring in between $1,500 and $1,700 per month rent. The lender always takes the smaller number—in this case, $1,500—to use in the loan calculations.

However, the lender will also credit your income picture with only 75 percent of this $1,500 income, or $1,125. This adjustment reflects the lender's estimate that a single family property may be vacant 25 percent of the time.

From this $1,125 figure, the lender deducts the new monthly loan payment on the distressed property—say that's $1,100—plus one-twelfth of the annual property taxes and insurance—say $200—for a total deduction of $1,300 ($1,100 plus $200). Thus, with a monthly income of $1,125 and monthly outlay of $1,300, the lender figures you'll have a negative cash flow of $175.

As the lender appraises your capacity, you'll have to show that after meeting all your other expenses, you'll have a surplus income of $175 per month to handle this negative cash flow.

Lenders who provide FHA and VA financing must base their loan approvals on a more detailed set of financial guidelines, which are prescribed by governmental authorities. For instance, the VA analyses are so inclusive that they take into consideration the residual income needed, after loan payments, for each individual family member according to the geographic region in which the family resides. See Chapter 7 for details.

With the loan-payment-to-income ratio pretty well set at no more than 33 percent of your net income, it's a good idea for you to be preapproved by a lender before you begin your search for property. Remember, to play it safe, make provision for the negative cash flow in your calculations if you intend not to occupy the property. By knowing the maximum loan amount you'll qualify for, you can direct your property search accordingly and save yourself a lot of time.

In other words, why look at property you can't afford? Or, on the other hand, why not buy as much as you can afford? From an investment point of view, that makes a lot of sense, doesn't it?

Collateral

Collateral is the asset pledged as security for a loan. For a home loan, the collateral is the property itself. As you saw earlier, except for certain government-backed loans, conventional lenders generally will not write a loan for more than 90 percent of the collateralized property's appraised value. The 10 percent margin between appraised value and loan value is the lender's cushion in the event of a foreclosure.

Through the use of an in-house or independent appraiser, the lender learns the market value of the property involved. The lender then determines the maximum loan possible based on that market appraisal.

Character

The kind of person you are—your character—is revealed somewhat in your credit report, your job stability, and the frequency of your changes of address. An applicant who's been gainfully employed for several years, hasn't moved about too frequently, and possesses a clean credit report has a lot of the "good" character traits sought by the lender. This type of borrower has a leg up on the credit-poor "frequent flyer," who can't seem to hold a steady job and changes addresses just about every season.

A credit report is a rather revealing statement of your character. It tells the banker the calibre of stores with which you have credit, the amount of your purchases, and your record of payment. If the lender sees too many 30-day or 60-day late payment entries, your character stature drops considerably. The same applies to "write-offs," outstanding judgments, bankruptcies, and foreclosures—they all play havoc with a lender's assessment of your character.

If your credit report is offensive to the lender, you can be sure you'll be asked to provide a cosigner for your loan, as discussed in Chapter 4. A cosigner is a guarantor who will be called on to make your loan payments in the event you fail to do so.

If a poor credit performance was caused by events beyond your control, type a letter to the lender explaining the difficulties. A prolonged sickness, a layoff from work, an accident—if any of those misfortunes contributed to your credit problems, bankers will be more forgiving in their judgment of you. However, if you are denied a loan because of poor credit, there's a federal law that mandates a lender to disclose the source of credit information that resulted in your loan rejection. It's called the Fair Credit Reporting Act.

Putting the Three Cs to Work

To get a "yes" from a lender . . .

- Present a decent credit report.

- Show that you have sufficient income to repay the loan.

- Show stability in your job and residences.

- Don't appear desperate for the money.

- Don't appear at the loan office dressed in "system-defiant" attire.

- Know everything about the property you're seeking to acquire.

- Project confidence that you'll make your payments promptly.

- Go to the loan office with all the necessary documentation completely and legibly prepared.

- Type a cover letter explaining what you're attempting to do.

- Treat the loan officer with dignity and respect.

- Give yourself plenty of time for the loan to be processed—at least 45 days before you need the money.

- Before you leave the meeting, make sure you understand all the details of the loan: terms, points, fees, up-front money, loan assumability, prepayment penalty, and the average time it takes to fund.

- Make sure the value of the property you're buying amply exceeds the amount of your requested loan.

Choose the Right Lender

In your quest for a loan, make sure you match up the right lender with the type of loan you want. For instance, if you're seeking home mortgage money, don't call on commercial banks that specialize in making business loans. Another example: Many lenders do not make vacant land loans. Therefore, make sure your research uncovers only those who do, if that's what you're looking for.

If you're looking for government-guaranteed FHA and VA loans, discussed thoroughly in Chapter 7, you can read the ads in the Yellow Pages of your phone directory. Lenders who participate in those programs usually advertise that they do so. If you can't find anyone in the Yellow Pages, call your nearest FHA (HUD) or VA office. The customer service person will send you a list of the approved lenders.

Besides being categorized according to the types of loans they make, lenders are additionally restricted in the maximum amount they can lend in certain situations. Many lenders, for instance, place a cap on the amount of a home loan they'll make even if that cap falls far short of their general loan-to-value ratio. Other lenders use different loan-to-value ratios for different types or price ranges of properties. For example, it's not uncommon for lenders to lower the loan-to-value ratio from 90 percent to 65 percent on high-priced, single family homes.

Secondary Mortgage Market

Some lenders restrict their loans to the maximum permitted by HUD. Those lenders usually sell their loan portfolio on the secondary mortgage market and then, for a fee, act as a collection agency.

The secondary mortgage market is very important to participating lenders. By selling their loans at a discount to agencies of that market, lenders recover most of their cash. With their recovered cash, they make more loans to new borrowers, which in turn generates more income in the form of fees and points. By repeating that process, potential borrowers are assured of an available reservoir of ready capital and lenders maintain a steady cash flow along with a profitable yield on funds loaned.

There are three agencies in the secondary mortgage market.

The Big Three

Federal National Mortgage Association (Fannie Mae)
This is a publicly held corporation that buys conforming FHA and VA first and second loans.

Federal Home Loan Mortgage Corporation (Freddie Mac)

This organization is run by the Federal Home Loan Bank, which regulates the savings and loan industry. With funds created by the sale of mortgage-backed bonds to large investors, this agency buys FHA and VA loans.

Government National Mortgage Corporation (Ginnie Mae)

This agency creates money to buy FHA and VA loans through the sale of certificates to investors. Those certificates pay them a safe, reliable monthly income consisting of principal and interest.

Those three agencies control billions of dollars worth of mortgages. With that enormous clout, they set the home loan requirements for a significant proportion of S&Ls. The agencies' rules, which are subject to change, involve loan-to-value ratios, loan amount limits, the exclusion of investor financing, the denial of cash out from refinancing, and borrower qualifications.

These agencies play a decisive role in the wonderful world of real estate. By being particularly effective in providing financing for first-time home buyers, the agencies continually enlarge the scope of real estate participants and provide a steady stream of customers for real estate entrepreneurs.

Among those customers are more future real estate wealth seekers. But, don't worry about too many players on the field! With all the tremendous opportunities out there, there's plenty for everyone. And keep in mind:

Anyone can become rich in real estate—anyone!

Always remember: You're learning to operate here in the most democratic business in the world—real estate. It's a democratic business, because it's one in which just about everyone can participate. But in order to participate, you need the assistance of lenders. It's by spreading around good old OPM that bankers give anyone who meets even minimum qualifications a crack at the action. It's really true; anyone can become rich in real estate—anytime.

So, after you've located the lender who's going to help make you wealthy, how do you converse with him or her? What questions do you ask? Here are a few helpful hints.

Some Important Topics to Discuss with Potential Lenders

In order to make a prudent choice of lenders, I suggest you make a comparison spreadsheet so that you can easily see what each has to offer. In the top margin of the following form, place the names of the lenders you're comparing. Along the left-hand side are items to complete for each potential lender so that you can compare apples with apples. (Not all of the topics on this form will pertain to every loan desired.)

Lenders Interviewed

Item			
Date	- - - - - - - -	- - - - - - - -	- - - - - - - -
Contact's Name	- - - - - - - -	- - - - - - - -	- - - - - - - -
Phone Number	- - - - - - - -	- - - - - - - -	- - - - - - - -
Makes Nonowner-Occupied Loans	- - - - - - - -	- - - - - - - -	- - - - - - - -
Fixed Rate Terms	- - - - - - - -	- - - - - - - -	- - - - - - - -
ARM Terms	- - - - - - - -	- - - - - - - -	- - - - - - - -
Points	- - - - - - - -	- - - - - - - -	- - - - - - - -
Application Fees	- - - - - - - -	- - - - - - - -	- - - - - - - -
FHA Terms	- - - - - - - -	- - - - - - - -	- - - - - - - -
VA Terms	- - - - - - - -	- - - - - - - -	- - - - - - - -
Loan-to-Value Ratio	- - - - - - - -	- - - - - - - -	- - - - - - - -
Down Payment Required	- - - - - - - -	- - - - - - - -	- - - - - - - -
Cash Out Okay on Refinance	- - - - - - - -	- - - - - - - -	- - - - - - - -
Prepayment Penalty	- - - - - - - -	- - - - - - - -	- - - - - - - -
Mortgage Assumption Requirements	- - - - - - - -	- - - - - - - -	- - - - - - - -
Rates Locked In	- - - - - - - -	- - - - - - - -	- - - - - - - -
Documents Needed to Apply (W-2s, Tax Returns, and so on)	- - - - - - - -	- - - - - - - -	- - - - - - - -

In an actual situation, after you've selected the lender that offers the best terms for your distressed property project, you'll submit a loan application. Refer to Chapter 4 for some tips on making yourself a desirable loan recipient. Your loan officer will tell you what else to include with the application—W-2 forms from your employer, previous income tax returns, a list of your bank accounts and investments, and so on.

When all the paperwork is received, a lengthy process follows to determine whether you qualify for the loan. The process is shortened however, if you followed my earlier advice and obtained your credit report and cleared any derogatory inquiries and errors from your credit record.

During the loan approval process, your "loan package" is assigned to an underwriter. This person analyzes your income and expenses to ensure that they conform to the lender's ratios as prescribed by the FNMA. Your checking and savings account balances will be verified and you'll be required to provide homeowner's insurance for the property whose policy value at least equals the loan value. The insurance must name the lender as co-insured.

Also during this process an appraisal is ordered. If the appraised value justifies the loan you're requesting and the underwriter verifies that your financial paperwork meets the bank's risk standards, the underwriter approves the loan and passes the application on to the lender's loan committee.

The loan committee usually consists of the loan department manager and another executive in the lending institution. They review the work of the underwriter. If everyone concurs, the committee members sign an approval. Shortly after that, you receive a letter from the underwriter stating the loan is approved.

In the next step, the lender prepares all the necessary loan documents—the note, trust deed or mortgage, and so on. You'll go to the lender's office again to sign those documents.

When you finally get your hands on the loan's paperwork, make sure you read and understand every word. You don't want surprises at your closing!

If items on the loan paperwork puzzle you, ask questions. The only "dumb question" is the one you don't ask!

Points to Ponder: The Fine Print of Loans

Once your interviews are completed and the loan papers are sitting in front of you, consider the items described here as you make up your mind.

Assumability and the Due-on-Sale Clause

A few years ago, when interest rates teetered around 17 percent, investors scoured the resale market to find properties with below-market freely assumable loans. Usually those loans were found being carried on old FHA and VA financed properties. Investors scooped up those deals because the assumability of their notes made the properties less costly to hold and very attractive to sell to future buyers.

With the use of a second trust deed—either taken back by the seller or some third party—the investor was able to purchase the property and assume, or take over, the low-interest first trust deed. Today, however, those freely assumable loans are few and far between.

The main stumbling block to any loan's assumability is the presence in the note of the "due-on-sale" clause, also called an "alienation" or "acceleration" clause. That clause gives the lender the power to call for full payment of the note long before its due date if certain events occur. Except for variable-rate loans, nearly all conventional loans contain some sort of acceleration clause. Typically, the clause reads as follows:

> In the event the trustor (borrower) should sell or agree to sell said property or any part thereof or any interest therein, the beneficiary (lender) may, at its option, declare the entire indebtedness secured hereby immediately due and payable.

Today, for a lender to agree to have a buyer assume an existing note, the buyer must be prepared to undergo as thorough an examination as the originator of the loan experienced. If the buyer's credit is poor, the assumption will be denied; if his or her income is deemed too small to quality for assumption, the buyer has to "buy down" the loan to a level he or she can afford.

Lenders' Right to Update an Assumed Note

Written into most notes is the right of the lender to charge an assumption fee and, at the lender's option, alter the note to reflect current rates and terms. The fees include a percentage of the loan balance along with escrow and title costs, a credit check, and recording charges.

If the buyer proves an acceptable risk to the lender, the buyer has to sign a "Substitution of Liability" document that releases the original maker of the note from all responsibility. The document will then be recorded.

In short:

When you apply for a loan assumption, be prepared to present yourself to the lender as if you were applying for a new loan.

But you can start smiling. Keep in mind that whether you qualify for a new loan or assume an old one, you're not really going into debt,

---

You're borrowing your way to wealth and independence.

Here's a variation on the old "Golden Rule" adage: The man with the gold makes the rules, like it or not. Conform to your banker's requirements. Until you become so wealthy that bankers will chase after you, you need them to pave your way to the top.

Subject-to Clause

Although an assumption agreement involves replacing the originator of the note with the buyer, "subject-to" transactions are easier. No substitution takes place; the original maker stays on the loan and retains ultimate responsibility for it. The buyer, without presenting the lender with any qualifications, merely takes over making the payments. There are no fees involved and the terms of the note remain intact. Subject-to transactions may be possible only in the absence of a due-on-sale clause in the note.

Prepayment Penalty

Some loans contain a clause that states the loan cannot be paid off within a certain time period—sometimes up to five years—without triggering a penalty. The penalty? Usually, it's about six months interest. Although present in some conventional loans, the clause is absent in FHA, VA, and variable-rate loans. Also, prepayment penalties are against the law in some states, so know your rights.

Knowing that loans very rarely go to term, the lenders who use the prepayment penalty do so in order to generate more income. But, avoid lenders who insist on the prepayment penalty. There are plenty of others out there who don't. The clause, usually hidden in fine print, will be a problem if you want to refinance within the prepayment period. Please . . .

Read and understand everything in a note before you sign it.

Points and Fees

By charging points and fees, banks generate a lot of operating cash and increase the yield on the money they lend. A *point* is 1 percent of the loan amount, and lenders—depending on the market—generally charge from one to three to originate a home loan.

Sometimes, you can trade points for interest rates. For example, you could offer to pay an extra point for a reduction in your interest rate or pay no points at all for a higher rate.

Fees encompass myriad expenses—everything from the cost of an appraisal to title insurance, escrow, credit reports, and other administrative charges.

Special Mortgages

The Wrap-Around or All-Inclusive Trust Deed

What is a wrap-around trust deed? As the name implies, it is a trust deed that "includes" prior assumable liens on the property. Because a wrap-around deed comes after other liens, it is basically a junior lien.

Junior is a general term that describes second or third trust deeds; a first trust deed is often called *senior*. When a trust deed "comes after" another encumbrance, it means that the deed's date of recording was subsequent to those of previously recorded liens.

A lien's date of recording becomes important in the event of a foreclosure. If the holder of a previously recorded lien initiates a foreclosure action, the holder of any junior lien must step in to protect his or her interest in the property. If the lien holder fails to act and the property is sold at a trustee sale, the senior lender will sell the property for an amount that covers the senior lien only, with no regard for the interest of the junior lienholder.

To prevent the evaporation of a junior lienholder's interest in a property, he or she must act early in the foreclosure process. The proper response by the junior lienholder is to

1. Make up any past due payments, along with late fees, and begin to make regular monthly payments in place of the defaulting trustor. Then the offended lender will stop the foreclosure action.

99

2. Begin a new foreclosure process to recover costs and protect his or her interests. Property sold at a trustee sale brought on by a junior lienholder is sold subject to the existing senior lien.

A wrap-around trust deed is usually written in an amount equal to the sales price less the down payment. The buyer receives title to the property along with an owner's policy of title insurance.

Why Should a Seller Use a Wrap?

There are several good reasons sellers may agree to your offer of creating a wrap-around deed:

- The seller wants monthly income from the sale proceeds rather than a lump sum of cash.

- The seller wants to avoid paying tax on the gain in one lump sum but prefers to spread that liability out over the term of the wrap mortgage.

- The seller has a low-interest assumable first trust deed that he or she doesn't want to merely "pass on" to a buyer and take back a conventional second trust deed.

- The seller wants to make a high effective rate of interest on the equity being lent to the buyer.

- The seller wants to save the buyer the expense and possible problem of refinancing the property.

- The seller wants to get the highest possible price for the property because he or she is offering the best terms.

A wrap-around trust deed could be an excellent way to finance a flip deal for a distressed property. If you're lucky enough to find a house with existing assumable loans and the seller agrees to a wrap, you can save the time and expense of securing new purchase financing.

Using a wrap, you can offer the seller a high rate of interest and a term just long enough to complete your project—possibly all in exchange for no down payment. A cash-poor seller with a distressed, hard-to-move property may go for such an arrangement. Point out that with a wrap-around trust deed the seller earns interest not only on the equity he or she lends you but also on the total value of the other liens. The following example illustrates how that windfall of interest works.

Example of a Wrap or All-Inclusive Trust Deed

Say a house is selling for $150,000. It has an assumable FHA mortgage in the amount of $100,000 at the fixed rate of 8 percent per year. The principal and interest payment is $660 per month. The seller wants a $20,000 down payment and will take back a trust deed for $130,000, the remainder of the sale price. The seller's total equity in the property is $50,000 ($150,000 less the $100,000 note).

Seller's Wrap Offer

$	150,000	Sale price
–	20,000	Down payment
$	130,000	Trust deed

The $130,000 paper the seller wants to carry back will be a wrap-around or all-inclusive trust deed. It will include two entities: the first mortgage of $100,000, and an "implied" junior trust deed of $30,000, the remainder of the seller's equity ($50,000 – $20,000 down payment). The entire $130,000 wrap-around trust deed will be secondary to the $100,000 first trust deed and will be recorded.

The terms of the wrap could be as follows:

- The loan will be amortized over 30 years but due in 10.

- The interest rate will be 11 percent per year.

- Monthly payments will be $1,192.00 interest only.

- The seller will make the monthly payments on the first from funds received from the buyer.

- Alternatively, the buyer will make payments to an escrow company that will then make the monthly payments to the holder of the first and remit the remainder of the buyer's payment to the seller.

Typical language of a wrap-around or all-inclusive trust deed reads like this:

> This is an all-inclusive second deed of trust, securing a note for $130,000 which includes within said sum, a $100,000 obligation of trustor to "X" bank. Beneficiary (Seller) hereby agrees with trustor (buyer) to discharge said $100,000 obligation in accordance with its terms and to hold trustor (buyer) harmless from any liability resulting from the failure of beneficiary (seller) to so discharge said obligation.

Find a good lawyer!

Here's a strong warning: *Always* use an experienced real estate attorney to draw up an all-inclusive trust deed and note. It's just too risky to try to use completely standardized forms because of the presence of too many variables. For instance, the rights of parties in the event of a foreclosure, the problem of escalating payments on an underlying variable-rate note, the possibility of a balloon payment on an underlying note coming due before the expiration of the wrap mortgage—all those kinds of knotty problems must be clearly ironed out by a qualified attorney.

Besides using a proper attorney, consult with the title company you propose to use. Because the title company will guarantee title, that firm has something to say about the form and content of the all-inclusive. Now, back to our example.

The Seller's Return Using the All-Inclusive

$	1,192	Monthly payment receivable
–	660	Payment on first trust deed
$	532	Net monthly payment received
$	6,384	Yearly return (12 × $532)
$	30,000	Implied junior lien in wrap ($130,000 – $100,000)

Yearly rate of return 21.3%

($6,384/$30,000)

The high return of 21.3 percent on $30,000 is the result of the fact that while the seller is in reality lending the buyer only $30,000, he's collecting interest on the $100,000 first trust deed as well.

Stable Mortgage

A new kind of mortgage has emerged in some areas of the country. Approved by Fannie Mae (Federal National Mortgage Association), the *stable mortgage* combines both fixed and variable rates in one note.

Distressed property entrepreneurs may find this type of long-term financing useful for a property they intend to use temporarily as a personal residence and subsequently to rent out. Besides the attractive low down payment required, it's a great idea to have financing that combines the stability of a fixed-rate loan and the "bargain" feature of a lower-interest, variable-rate loan.

The stable mortgage has the following two options:

- The borrower may have the lender write 75 percent of the loan amount at a fixed rate and 25 percent at a variable rate. The variable-rate portion would be recalculated every year. This option requires only a 5 percent down payment from the borrower.

- The loan would be divided in half. One half would be set at a fixed rate and the other at a variable one. To get this option, the borrower would put 10 percent down.

This is another attempt by lenders to give home buyers a less volatile monthly mortgage payment. For instance, under the first option, a $100,000 loan would be cast as follows:

$	645	Monthly payment of $75,000 fixed-rate loan at 9¾% per month
+	183	Monthly payment of $25,000 variable-rate loan at 8% per month
$	828	Total payment each month for the first year

The same loan amount under the second option would be

$	430	Monthly payment of $50,000 fixed-rate loan at 9¾% per month
+	367	Monthly payment of $50,000 variable-rate at 8%
$	797	Total monthly payment for the first year

In both instances, the "fixed" portion of the loan would offer some stability and result in smaller payment fluctuations.

The stable mortgage is a wonderful example of how old ideas are mingled to form a new concept. Real estate is always in a state of flux. To keep abreast of all the changes, you must attend lectures and read industry newspaper and magazine articles along with the latest books. You never know when an idea will spark your interest and set you on another money-making venture.

As an example, a few years ago I just happened to attend a lecture given by an attorney. He was extolling the money-making virtues of converting apartments to condos or co-ops. By the end of the lecture, I was convinced that that's what I should do with the units I owned. Later, I did. And, it was one of the most lucrative operations I ever completed. Yet, before I heard the lecture, I had never thought of it!

The Adjustable-Rate Mortgage

Especially for a flip project, the adjustable-rate mortgage (ARM) is an advantage for distressed property investors because this mortgage features a low initial interest rate. This lower rate makes it easier to qualify for the loan and significantly cuts the costs of holding the property to sale.

Because all adjustable-rate loans are assumable, a potential buyer of your rehabbed project can benefit as well by buying during the low initial rate and avoid the time and expense of securing new financing.

As the name implies, this instrument's interest rate is not fixed. Starting with a below-market "teaser" rate, it provides for periodic changes—up or down—over its term. When you're an investor doing a flip project within a year, the upward fluctuation of the ARM interest rate shouldn't trouble you.

The Index and the Spread

The interest rate change depends on two separate entities:

- The "index" to which it is tied

- The "spread" or "margin" over the index

Both the index and spread are defined in the mortgage note. Many lenders in the West tie their rates to the 11th District Cost of Funds as the index.

The spread is the number of points, usually between 2¼ and 2¾ more than the index, that they'll charge the borrower. For instance, if the 11th District Cost of Funds is pegged at 7½ percent and the spread is 2½ points, the interest rate charged will be 10 percent.

The Monthly Payment Cap and Negative Amortization

In a variable-rate loan, the interest rate is usually recalculated every six months. But in order to keep the monthly payment from escalating too high too fast, most notes contain a monthly payment "cap" of 7 percent per year. The presence of the cap, although it helps to keep the monthly payments more predictable, can result in *negative amortization*. That's a fancy way of saying the loan's principal balance will increase rather than decrease. Let's see why.

105

Say the current monthly loan payment on a variable-rate note is $1,000. When the time arrives to recast the monthly payment, the highest increase possible with a 7 percent "cap" would be $70 (0.07 × $1,000), resulting in a new monthly payment of $1,070.

However, suppose the interest rate increases to an amount that requires an additional $100 per month to pay the principal and interest? That would raise the monthly payment from $1,000 to $1,100. But hold on. Didn't you just see that the 7 percent cap limited the increase to no more than $70 (7 percent of $1,000)? Well, that's true; the lender will have to abide by the "cap rate" as indicated in the note. So, instead of asking you to make your monthly payment for $1,100, the lender has to settle for $1,070.

What happens to the $30 difference between what the lender is entitled to charge you and what you actually pay? That $30 is added to the principal balance of your loan. Your loan, then, does not decrease after your monthly payment—it increases by $30 instead! This is *negative amortization* at work.

If you choose to make the higher payment of $1,100, of course, you can. That will eliminate racking up a $30-per-month increase in your loan balance.

The beginning low rate of interest on this type of loan impacts the buyer's borrowing qualifications. Because lenders tie the monthly loan payment to a percentage of the buyer's net monthly income, the smaller that note payment, the easier it is for the lender to qualify the buyer for the loan. Recently, Fannie Mae (Federal National Mortgage Association) tightened the rules participating lenders must use to qualify buyers for adjustable-rate mortgages.

Heretofore, if an adjustable-rate mortgage had a beginning "teaser" rate of say 6 percent, that would be the rate used by the lender to calculate the borrower's affordable monthly loan payment. No more.

Now, no matter how low the beginning rate may be, lenders must qualify the borrower as if the rate were 7 percent. (Of course, if the stated beginning rate is over 7 percent, that would be the one used to qualify the borrower.)

Another new rule: The minimum qualifying rate can be higher than 7 percent in some cases if the mortgage

- Has a 2 percent annual cap

- Has a term greater than 15 years

- Has a loan-to-value ratio of more than 75 percent

If the loan has these three features, the borrower must be qualified at the *maximum* interest rate he or she could be charged at the beginning of the second year.

Lifetime Cap

Besides a monthly payment cap, most variable-rate loans have a lifetime interest cap that defines the highest rate possible. Conversely, these loans also have a minimum rate, because it is conceivable that the rate could go down as well.

Why Use a Variable-rate Loan?

There are some very good reasons to use variable-rate loans. The following are some of the more obvious ones:

- Because of the below-market beginning rate, the loan is easier to qualify for.

- Variable-rate loans open the housing market to a larger number of people. An expanding market is especially useful for distressed property entrepreneurs. The more people in the market for your product, the faster and more frequently you can perform flip deals and churn profits.

- The notes are assumable with the lender's approval.

- The notes can be paid off anytime without incurring a penalty, thereby making refinancing easier.

- The below-market interest rate is great for investors who need low carrying costs in flip deals—buy, fix, sell.

- Appreciation might wipe out the negative amortization.

- If the monthly payments become too high, it may be possible to refinance an ARM with a new, low "teaser" rate of another variable loan and begin the process all over again.

- Lenders are more lenient with the qualifications of borrowers applying for variable-rate loans because they like to issue them.

In the wonderful world of real estate, it's always better to safely use as much OPM as possible. I used the word *safely* to stress that you should never encumber yourself with loan payments you cannot afford.

By using OPM at the lowest rate possible via a variable-rate loan, you'll increase the yield on your investment. The greater your yield, the more you'll be able to re-invest. The more you re-invest, the greater the number of people you'll employ to improve your properties. When we all work and invest in real estate, America prospers!

Real Estate Settlement and Procedures Act

In years past, first-time home buyers were often stunned by the fees that they unknowingly amassed during escrow. Lender's points, title insurance, appraisals, credit reports, escrow charges, and myriad other "garbage" fees were revealed to buyers only when escrow was about to close. Those expenses, often amounting to thousands of dollars, forced the buyer, at the last moment, to scramble around to raise the cash to pay for them. In some instances, those buyers unable to do so, had to lose their purchase, which injured the seller's position as well.

In 1974, that insane practice came to a screeching halt: Congress enacted the Real Estate Settlement and Procedures Act (RESPA).

That law mandated federally affiliated lenders to issue to the borrower a good faith estimate of all possible costs within three days of receiving the loan application.

Now, when you make a real estate purchase and apply for a loan, the costs involved are no longer a mystery. Thus, another loose end in the real estate business has been corrected, making it easier for us to operate with our eyes wide open.

Finding the right lender, asking the right questions, preparing your loan application, and knowing how to get a "yes" from the lender are all integral parts of the glorious world of real estate. When you master the task of getting all the OPM you want, you'll be well on your way to your world of opulence and security.

The U.S. Government: Your Friend in Deed!

The main intent of this book is to encourage you to take advantage of the incredible opportunities that distressed properties offer. As earlier chapters revealed, the major obstacle to making your first deal is scratching up that first down payment. Chapters 4 and 5 dealt with this issue, but there's an additional source of funding to get you started: government-backed loans from the Federal Housing Administration (FHA) and the Veterans Administration (VA). Remember, though, that this type of financing is available only to purchase property you will occupy.

Conventional loans currently offer interest rates that are very close to those of government loans, so today the principal reason for using government-backed financing for the purchase of distressed property is the low down payment requirement.

Consider this advantage: Conventional lenders will lend you no more than 90 percent of the appraised value of the property; the FHA will lend you 95 percent, and a VA loan could possibly bring that amount to 100 percent. This advantage is substantial if you're a cash-strapped, first-time investor. Thus, instead of the $12,500 down payment required for a conventional loan on a $125,000 property, an FHA borrower would need just $6,250 for that property, and a VA borrower might need no down payment at all! Such government-backed loans take much of the "scraping" out of scraping up a down payment.

FHA: Federal Housing Administration

Since its inception in 1934, more than 17 million American families have used FHA financing, proving it to be one of the most beneficial government sponsored programs ever devised. Although the maximum loan amounts offered vary region to region, the FHA appears to offer many people just about the right loan—especially for those at the entry level of housing. Currently, the FHA is processing 700,000 loans per year.

FHA is under the auspices of the U.S. Department of Housing and Urban Development (HUD). You can locate your local FHA branch by calling the HUD regional office in your area. It's listed under the "U.S. Government" heading in the white pages of your phone directory.

FHA: Lender Guarantor

The FHA itself does not make loans. Its banking affiliates do the lending. What FHA does is make it safe for their lenders to lend. It does that by guaranteeing 25 percent of the loan amount so that their bank and S&L affiliates are at risk for only 75 percent of the money they put into the marketplace.

That 25 percent guarantee provides an excellent cushion for lenders in the event of a foreclosure. As a contrast, under conventional or non-FHA financing, the lender normally requires up to 20 percent down payment. On a house appraised at $125,000, that 20 percent amounts to $25,000 and implies a mortgage of $100,000. In the event of a foreclosure, all the bank has to sell the property for in order to recover its loan would be $100,000 plus foreclosure fees—a fairly safe predicament.

But not as safe a predicament as that of the FHA-guaranteed lender, in spite of the fact that his down payment requirement is much less. Let me explain: FHA financing requires about 5 percent down; specifically, 3 percent of the first $25,000 of the appraised value and 5 percent of the remainder up to the loan limit, which varies by region (currently $124,750 here in Southern California). On the $125,000 house in our example, the FHA-required down payment would be $5,750, figured as follows:

$	125,000	Appraised value
	750	The first $25,000 × 3%
+	5,000	The remainder $100,000 × 5%
$	5,750	Total down payment
$	119,250	Loan Amount ($125,000 – $5,750)

Without the 25 percent FHA loan guarantee, the bank, with only a $5,750 down payment, would be exposing itself to a dangerous $119,250 resale situation in the event of a foreclosure. However, because the FHA guarantees the lender 25 percent of the loan, in this case, $29,812 (25 percent of $119,250), all the bank would have to sell the $125,000 property for would be $89,438 ($119,250 – $29,812) plus foreclosure fees. That's a pretty safe situation.

What makes the FHA deal even safer for the lender is the fact that the FHA, under a foreclosure action, will usually pay off the lender's note in its entirety, take over the property, and proceed with the foreclosure, freeing the lender from any further responsibility. That's why lenders love the FHA.

Recent Policy Change

Recently, to the dismay of many first-time home buyers, the FHA boosted the cash needed to buy a home. Up to the date of this new policy, the borrower could add all the escrow closing costs plus the FHA-required federal mortgage insurance premium to the loan amount. That feature added significantly to the desirability of FHA financing, because it lowered the amount of cash needed by the buyer.

Now, the FHA says that the buyer must make a cash payment of 43 percent of the closing costs at the time of purchase and pay a monthly mortgage insurance premium at the yearly rate of 0.5 percent of the loan amount. Truthfully, we're not talking really big bucks here! Moreover, the FHA contends that the added cash is too small an amount to deter prospective home buyers. But here's why the agency changed the rule.

In some areas of the country, home prices have declined. As a result, there have been too many instances where FHA property owners saw their 5 percent equity erode away to nothing. Unable to recoup their down payment in a sale, many homeowners simply walked away from their property, leaving the FHA with foreclosures to sell. Now, with a greater cash requirement to purchase, the FHA hopes owners will be less inclined to renege on their obligations and make the necessary commitments to hang on to their property.

How to Get an FHA Loan: Mortgage Brokers

FHA loans are normally handled by mortgage brokers. *Mortgage brokers* are professionals whose expertise lies in matching the loan desired with the proper lender.

With hundreds of lenders to choose from, these brokers know at any given time which lenders are doing which FHA programs. It doesn't directly cost you any money to use a mortgage broker. The broker's fees are paid for by the lender.

Mortgage brokers are listed in the Yellow Pages of your phone directory.

The mortgage broker takes your application, does a credit check on you, determines whether you're qualified for the loan you seek, places the loan package with the most appropriate lender, and then monitors the whole process right up to the close of escrow.

The FHA itself, on the other hand, is primarily a policy-making organization. It's set up to review loan applications, hire or train appraisers, regulate property inspections, and certify those lenders willing to participate in their programs.

Getting right down to basics, the following is an adaptation of the form the FHA advocates for determining the income qualifications of an applicant. Why don't you plug your numbers into the analysis and see whether you qualify for an FHA loan?

How to Figure FHA Income Qualification

Monthly Income

Gross monthly income	$ _____	
Less Federal Income Tax	− _____	
Net Monthly Income	= _____	This is A

Monthly Expenses

House payments of principal and interest	$ _____	
Real Estate Taxes	+ _____	
Homeowners Insurance	+ _____	
FHA Mortgage Insurance	+ _____	
Utilities	+ _____	
Total Housing Expense	= _____	This is B

*B divided by A equals a percentage, which ideally should not exceed 38%.

Fixed Obligations

Total monthly housing expenses	$ _____	
Total of other monthly expenses that will continue over one year	+ _____	
Social security deduction	+ _____	
Monthly State Income Tax	+ _____	
Total monthly fixed obligations	= _____	This is C

*C divided by A equals a percentage, which ideally should not exceed 53%.

If the actual percentages exceed the ones quoted here, the FHA may, under special circumstances, still grant the loan.

Special Features of FHA

Following are some specifics to consider when you're thinking about applying for an FHA loan.

Owner Occupancy

The property must be owner occupied. Even when the property is a duplex, triplex or four-unit apartment house, one of the units must be occupied by the owner.

Impound Account

FHA requires an impound account—sometimes called an *escrow account*—into which the borrower, besides the monthly principal and interest payment, must make a monthly payment toward the real estate taxes, homeowners insurance, and the FHA insurance.

Closing Costs

Fifty-seven percent of the closing costs can be added to the loan. Forty-three percent must be paid up front in cash. However, it's possible to have the seller pay all or part of your closing costs, depending on the deal you make.

Loan Amount Limits/Down Payment

Maximum loan amounts vary from region to region. The down payment is about 5 percent of the appraised value, not the purchase price.

Mortgage Broker

FHA loans are usually arranged by a mortgage broker; however, a few banks and S&Ls handle them directly.

Assumability

FHA loans are no longer freely assumable. Buyers must prove that their income is sufficient and must possess a good credit history in order to assume an FHA loan.

Interest Rates

FHA interest rates are generally lower than those of conventional lenders.

Property Standards

The property being financed must meet certain minimum FHA standards. Some sellers are reluctant to accept a deal with the contingency that the buyers obtain FHA financing. The reason? Property financed by FHA affiliated lenders must undergo a thorough physical inspection. All the noted defects must be corrected before the close of escrow or the funding will be denied. FHA inspectors go through every inch of the property, inside and out.

Their investigation, among other things, includes the following:

- Safe electrical wiring and adequate plumbing

- Weatherstripping

- Proper number of electrical outlets in each room

- Leak-free roof

- Adequate caulking

- Proper insulation

- Proper ventilation

- Attractive painting

- Proper exterior drainage

Many distressed properties you'll encounter will need at least some repairs to meet these safety standards—repairs that must be completed by the seller before the close of escrow to qualify for the FHA funding. You may wonder how to reconcile the fact that the property is distressed on your way into the deal and no longer distressed on your way out.

Understand one important point. The repairs required to meet the FHA codes most likely will fall short of the repairs and enhancements you'll have to make to compete with your best comparables. In effect, you're still buying a distressed property; it's just not *quite* as distressed! The sellers will address the "hidden defects"—faulty wiring, inadequate plumbing, and so on. You'll make the "flash and dash" changes—the carpeting, window treatments, landscaping, and so on—that will attract subsequent buyers.

When you, a budding distressed-property investor, approach sellers, you're in the driver's seat. Because the sellers don't have a bevy of anxious buyers vying to purchase their property, you can by and large dictate the terms of the deal. Here's what you do:

1. Get the sellers to accept the idea of FHA financing as a condition of sale.

2. The sellers' acceptance of FHA financing means that they will have to make all the necessary repairs to meet the FHA codes. It becomes their problem to solve, not yours.

Points

Buyers are permitted to pay the lender only one point, 1 percent of the loan amount. If the lender charges more than that, then the seller must bear the additional cost.

Appraisal

The loan amount is based on the FHA appraisal, not the purchase price. Therefore, if you're seeking 95 percent financing and the FHA appraisal is lower than your purchase price, you'll have to come up with additional cash for the difference in order to complete the purchase.

Maximum Income

Remember: There is no maximum income standard for most FHA loans. Even if you earn over $100,000 per year, you can still qualify for some programs. FHA can and does finance just about everyone over 18, regardless of marital status or length of employment, as long as the person is creditworthy and can show verifiable proof of income.

Types of FHA Loans

203-b

The 203-b is the most popular FHA loan, composing about 80 percent of its total lending output. It's a very simple loan: You make a cash outlay of 3 percent of the first $25,000 of the appraised value, 5 percent of the remainder, and 43 percent of the closing costs. The remainder of the closing costs will be added to your loan. The FHA does permit the seller to pay all or part of the closing costs, if that's part of the purchase deal. The mortgage, which if granted runs for 30 years, can be at a fixed or variable rate, is assumable with lender approval, and has no prepayment penalty.

The following are points to remember about the 203-b:

- The 95 percent loan amount is based on the FHA appraisal, not the purchase price.

- If the purchase price is higher than the appraisal, unless the seller will accept the appraised value, the buyer must come up with the difference in cash.

- There is a maximum loan limit.

- The property must be owner-occupied.

3-2 Option

The 3-2 option is a new, low down payment mortgage that recently became available. It permits borrowers to use only 3 percent of their own money as part of the 5 percent down payment. The other 2 percent may originate as a gift from a family member or as a grant from a nonprofit organization. The program was established to aid renters with jobs paying enough money to meet monthly debt services, but whose savings were insufficient to meet the normal FHA down payment requirements. Under this plan, the borrower can use up to 33 percent of his or her monthly income for loan payments.

119

Title I Loans

This program, subtitled "The Home Improvement Loan," permits homeowners to borrow up to $17,500, amortized over 15 years, to pay for certain house repairs. Although the interest rate may be a little less than that charged under a conventional home improvement loan, the lender's fees are quite high. Most affiliates participating in this program charge from 6 to 10 points—$1,050 to $1,750—for a $17,500 loan. The points charged are deducted from the loan proceeds at the time of funding.

However, this is a great loan for homeowners who are short of cash and lean of equity. Because of the FHA guarantee, lenders do not base the loan amount on the borrower's equity in the property. As a matter of fact, a homeowner can get this loan with no equity at all.

What the lenders require of the borrowers are a good credit history and sufficient income to meet the additional monthly payment.

When you apply for this loan, you have to submit a detailed list of the improvements to be made, along with their approximate costs. Although most ordinary repairs such as painting, carpeting, and landscaping are permissible, luxury items, such as pools and spas, are not.

You generally have six months to make the repairs, after which time the lender will appear to verify their completion. If, for some legitimate reason, you encounter difficulty in meeting the six-month timetable, the lender will grant you a six-month extension. Another valuable feature about this loan is that it can be funded in about three weeks. Be prepared, however, to provide the lender with the usually required personal documents that accompany any other loan application.

Title I lenders usually advertise the fact that they make such loans. They're listed in your local phone directory. Or, you can call your regional FHA office, and they'll send you a list of their current Title I lender affiliates.

203(k) Programs

Throughout my career in real estate, with the exception of investing in or building new projects, I've stuck to the practice of purchasing distressed properties in need of cosmetic repair only. However, for those of you willing and able to take on a more intense project, one involving structural alterations, remodeling, and other major improvements, there's an FHA program available that you may find useful: 203(k). However, the cost of repairs under the 203(k) plan must exceed $17,500—the Title I loan limit.

Sometimes, when a home buyer decides to buy a property in need of complete modernization, first he or she has to obtain purchase financing, then alterations financing, and finally, permanent financing. That can be very costly and time consuming.

Under the 203(k) plan, the borrower gets only one 30-year loan either at a fixed or a variable rate. The loan amount is based on the projected value of the property after the work is completed and is composed of two elements: the amount needed for purchase and the amount needed for rehab. When the loan is funded, a rehabilitation escrow account is established to hold the money earmarked for repairs. As the repairs are completed, the lender or his or her agent authorizes payment from that account.

Another nice feature about the 203(k) concerns mortgage payments. Up to six monthly mortgage payments can be included in the rehab portion of the loan. Those funds, sitting in the escrow account, will be withdrawn by the lender as the monthly mortgage payments come due. The loan amount available under the 203(k) plan is calculated as the *lesser* of either of these:

- The as-is value of the property before rehab plus the cost of rehab

- 110 percent of the expected market value on completion

The maximum you can borrow for owner-occupied property is 95 percent of the estimated value in either alternative. For investor-owned property, the loan amount, based on either alternative drops down to 85 percent. However, if the investor, after rehab, intends to sell the property to a buyer acceptable by HUD, the investor will be able to get a loan in excess of 85 percent of the project's value. For further information about this or any other FHA plan, you can call your regional HUD office or write to the following:

> U.S. Dept. of Housing and Urban Development
> 7th and D St. S.W.
> Washington, D.C. 20410-3000

> HUD's phone number is 1-800-733-4663.

VA: Veterans Administration

The Veterans Administration (VA) program was created in 1944 to give returning World War II veterans a new start in life. It was the government's way of thanking so many men and women who sacrificed so much. To give them help in acquiring a house, the U.S. government backed them up when they sought a home loan from a bank or S&L. How did the government do this? By guaranteeing the lender a portion of the loan, thereby reducing the lender's risk.

Actually, today the VA guarantees 50 percent of a loan of $45,000 or less. For loans of more than $45,000 the department guarantees 40 percent of the loan amount, or $36,000, whichever is higher.

It has proven to be a very practical program in two essential ways: It has spurred the housing industry, and it has helped veterans acquire homes.

Zero Down

So, why not have the United States as your silent partner in your initial real estate venture? If you're a qualified veteran without enough cash to place a down payment on a house, the VA program helps you enter the real estate market with zero cash down. That's right, *no* cash down!

There are some limitations, of course. For instance, to buy with nothing down, the price you pay for the property cannot exceed $184,000, the current maximum VA loan. But, everything considered, the VA program is a financial bonanza for all veterans—especially those at the entry level of the housing market.

How the Government Defines "Veteran"

Any male or female who served 90 days active duty in the armed forces prior to September 8, 1980, and was discharged under conditions other than dishonorable is eligible for VA benefits. For people who served after September 8, 1980, the active duty requirement is lengthened to 24 months. They too must have been discharged under conditions other than dishonorable to be VA qualified.

The VA Advantage

With a current 7.5 percent fixed interest rate, VA rates are among the best buy on the market today. They are easier to qualify for and have a 30-year term. VA loans are assumable—even by non-veterans, as long as they meet the income requirements and have good credit. To play it safe, make sure the buyer signs a formal assumption agreement releasing you from any responsibility for the loan. If you don't, the VA—which acts just as the FHA with respect to its loans—will come after you if the subsequent owners lose the property through foreclosure, and the trustee sale fails to bring in enough money to cover the lender's liens. The VA can do that even in states that have antideficiency laws that prohibit conventional lenders from recovering losses beyond the value of the property itself.

VA Monthly Net Income Requirements

The VA monthly net income requirement is very detailed. Starting with the combined monthly gross income, the monthly net income is arrived at by deducting the federal, state, and local income taxes along with social security tax. Then, deducted from that sum are the housing and long-term fixed expenses, such as car loans and furniture payments. The amount remaining is what the VA refers to as "family support" money. That number must be a certain prescribed amount that varies according to the region in which you live and the number of people in your family. Then, the VA goes one step further.

The VA has determined that the total housing expense plus fixed expenses, divided by the net monthly income, must not exceed 41 percent of your net income. If it does, the applicant must satisfactorily explain why. Any VA lender will be glad to send you a brochure outlining the exact current guidelines.

VA Fees

There are several charges connected with a VA loan. Some are paid for by the veteran, and some must be borne by the seller. As you may guess, the biggest fees go to the lender. Based on a percentage of the loan amount, all the fees as currently priced are divided as follows:

Lender Fees Paid by the Veteran

Loan origination fee	1 percent.
Funding fee	1.25 percent. This sum can be added to the loan amount as long as it does not raise the balance to an amount over $184,000, the current VA loan limit

Lender Fees Paid by the Seller

Discount points	3 percent. (Depending on the market, the discount points range anywhere from 0 to 5.)

Nonlender Fees Paid by the Veteran

Recording of the trust deed and grant deed

Credit report

Lender's title policy

Tax and insurance impounds

Appraisal fee

Nonlender Fees Paid by the Seller

All escrow fees

Tax Service

County and local transfer taxes, if any

Title policy

Broker's commissions

Payoff of existing liens and encumbrances

Note: Although the veteran can negotiate to have the seller pay for all or any of the veteran's costs, he or she cannot, under any circumstances, negotiate to assume any of the seller's costs.

The VA, like the FHA, does not normally make loans directly. Rather, the VA has lender affiliates who do so. In certain areas where no VA affiliate is available, the VA then acts as a direct lender.

VA Appraisal

The *appraisal* is the basis on which VA loans are made. If it comes in at a figure equal to the purchase price but not higher than $184,000, then the veteran, with the exception of closing costs, will have a no-down deal.

If the purchase price exceeds the loan limit of $184,000, the veteran can ask the seller to carry back a second trust deed for the difference. However, the veteran must put up cash in the amount of 25 percent of the difference between the $184,000 loan limit and the purchase price.

Example of a Second Trust Deed Situation

$	190,000	Purchase price
−	184,000	Maximum VA loan
	6,000	Amount not covered by loan
−	1,500	25% cash by veteran
$	4,500	Second trust deed carried back by seller

The veteran ends up with a VA first trust deed of $184,000 and a second trust deed of $4,500 carried back by the seller. Because the very existence of the VA is dependant on its ability to help veterans, that organization will literally bend over backward to produce an appraisal equal to the purchase price. The veteran can assist the appraiser in this task by doing some homework:

- Make the appraiser aware of the appraisal you need.

- Show the appraiser comps that support your purchase price.

- Accompany the appraiser on the appraisal and make it as easy as possible for him or her to do the job.

Affordable Housing:
The Resolution Trust Corporation

The newest government-created, real estate involved agency is the Resolution Trust Corporation (RTC). Although primarily concerned with the disposal of large repossessed complexes using local auctions, RTC has sold a formidable number of single family homes since its inception. To facilitate sales, the government has set up a special affordable housing program to accommodate buyers whose combined incomes are as low as $22,000.

The income cap varies by region and family size; however, the general rule of thumb is that to qualify, you cannot earn more than 115 percent of the area's median income. The homes sold under the affordable program must have a market value of $67,500 or less.

To find out when an auction is going to take place in your particular area, you can call 1-800-RTC-3006 or, you can call your closest RTC office. There are regional headquarters located in Kansas City, Dallas, Denver, and Atlanta. Sales offices are located in Phoenix, Arizona; Houston and San Antonio, Texas; Tulsa Oklahoma; Tampa, Florida; Costa Mesa, California; Somerset, New Jersey; King of Prussia, Pennsylvania; Egan, Minnesota; and Elk Grove Village, Illinois.

Before an intended auction, the RTC operates conventions where you can find out whether you qualify to participate in the affordable housing program. You can also get a list of available houses, their addresses, inspection dates, and the rules of the auction procedure.

I urge you to use the government as your "Friend in Deed." The programs described in this chapter are designed to assist cash-poor people in the acquisition of housing.

Although the government programs I've described in this chapter are among the most popular, there are many other, lesser known ones. If you have a particular financing problem that does not fit the mold of the programs given here, consult some FHA lenders. Explain your problem to them, and they may be able to point you toward a government package that will precisely accommodate your particular need.

Nonjudicial Foreclosure

If you know the foreclosure laws of your state, and if you can patiently ingratiate yourself with people under duress, you'll have two of the essential attributes necessary to make money in foreclosures.

Unlike some other distressed property deals, foreclosures, burdened with so many individual fiscal differences, defy the use of any formulas or standards to predetermine their profitability. Therefore, each project must be judged on its own merits. The only thing you can possibly do beforehand is to decide the percentage of profit you'd like to make on your invested capital.

A nonjudicial foreclosure action is begun by filing a document called the notice of default. It is filed by the lender-appointed trustee. Your pursuit of notices of default is the first action you take to reach your ultimate goal of purchasing a distressed foreclosed property.

How to Locate Notices of Default and Begin Negotiations in Foreclosure Deals

Locating Notices of Default

I've used three principal sources to find notices of default:

1. *County recorder's office.* Usually, all the notices of default are bound together and are readily available to any interested party. First look at the date the notice was filed: Is there enough time remaining in the reinstatement period (described in a moment) to complete a deal?

2. *Professional journals.* Newspapers that cater to the legal profession contain notices of default listed along with numerous other legal filings such as bankruptcies, divorces, and probate sales. Check your metropolitan phone directory for the names of such papers in your area. Subscription rates are usually reasonable.

3. *Professional "list compilers."* These firms employ people to search the records of the county recorder's office to compile all the information needed for different kinds of prevailing legal actions, notices of default included. Usually, the clerks in the recorder's office know those firms and will be glad to give you their phone numbers.

If you have such a firm in your area, subscribe to their service. They'll provide you with fast, up-to-date, bimonthly or monthly listings that save you a lot of research time.

How to Confront Foreclosure Victims

When you attempt to purchase properties in foreclosure, it's important that you give the owners in default the impression that you're placing their interests and their welfare above your own. If they sense that you're "using them" or "manipulating them," they'll rebel and you won't have a deal. You must be sensitive to their feelings, ethical in your actions and completely impassive to the anger that they may inveigh on you. Here are some hints to keep in mind when you're confronting the owners:

- Don't appear before them in intimidating attire—no three-piece suits, diamond rings, or other expensive jewelry.

- Smile. Try to please them with friendship, in spite of their resistance to you.

- Be courteous even if they are belligerent.

- Don't get too familiar. Use "Mr." and "Mrs." when you address them.

- Use gentle persuasion by emphasizing only what's best for them.

- Don't look on them as "losers."

- Don't contradict them; counter their thoughts with factual information.

- Even though they may put you off, waiting for a miracle, ask them for permission to stay in touch, just in case.

- If the foreclosure victims are separated or filing for divorce, you must do the following: Never take sides. Don't pry. Get both parties to sign all documents, no matter what they may say. At the conclusion of the sale, give each party a separate check for one-half of their equity.

Cause of Foreclosure

The principal cause of foreclosure is the erosion of the owner's equity in the property. The erosion can be created by

- placing too many loans on the property in order to raise cash. Then, the loss of employment, a severe lengthy illness, a business failure, or an expensive divorce cuts off the funds needed to make the additional payments.

- the temporary cessation of appreciation that builds equity in the property through higher market value.

The number of people who are delinquent with their home loan payments is now the highest it has been since 1986. A soft real estate market and a high delinquency rate has set the stage for an impending bonanza of foreclosures.

Lenders View Foreclosures as an Action of Last Resort

Conventional lenders really don't want to foreclose on a property. The only time a lender resorts to foreclosure is when the borrower is no longer able or willing to adhere to some kind of repayment schedule.

Professional lenders subscribe to this formula: Find out the reason for the borrowers' delinquencies and then help them forge a solution. The lenders' collection departments, staffed with people trained to be sensitive to borrowers' needs, regard foreclosure only as a last desperate act.

Most of the time, potential foreclosure candidates—habitually delinquent borrowers—are first-time property owners. They generally are not fully aware of the dire effects their cavalier attitude toward making payments will have on their credit record. If they're indeed facing a fiscal crisis, they don't know that they should contact their lenders, explain the situation, and ask for help. Lenders do themselves an injustice here. If they informed their borrowers of their basic "foreclosure-avoidance" policy, they'd make life easier for themselves and their borrowers.

In an attempt to avoid foreclosure, lenders can aid their borrowers in the following ways:

- They can modify the loan to require smaller payments.

- They can give the borrowers time to sell the property.

- They can accept a deed-in-lieu. (More on that later.)

- They can adjust the current repayment schedule.

However, as so often happens, when all of the above fail, when the doors are finally shut, the lender is forced to foreclose.

If the lenders have trust deeds on the properties, in many states they can choose to foreclose in either of two ways:

- They can use the court system and foreclose as if they held mortgages.

- They can avert the court system and foreclose under the terms of the trust deeds.

Under the first option, lenders must file a suit against the borrowers. The court will then do two things. It will order an auction of the property and will appoint receivers to conduct that auction. The advantage for the lenders here is that if the auction doesn't bring in enough money to cover their losses, in some states they can go after the borrowers for the difference. That's called *seeking a deficiency judgment*. The disadvantage is that the whole judicial process takes a long time.

Subsequent purchasers of property foreclosed that way will find themselves in jeopardy. Why? Because the original owners of the property have the right to come back and redeem it within one year of the sale.

However, if the lenders feel as though the property, after sale, will bring in enough to cover their potential losses, they will choose to foreclose without using the court system—the second option. Generally speaking, most lenders will use that nonjudicial approach, because it's faster and less costly. It's true that they may relinquish the right to a deficiency judgment, but in today's market, they can usually recover enough of their losses to where that's not an issue.

With property foreclosed under the nonjudicial system, the former owners do not have any redemption rights after the trustee sale.

An exception to the general deficiency judgment rule is as follows: If the property involved has an FHA or VA loan, the U.S. government can seek a deficiency judgment under any circumstance, even in states that normally prohibit conventional lenders from doing so.

Now, let's go through the generally applied foreclosure process and learn how it operates. Remember, each state has its own particular laws; become familiar with those of your state.

The Nonjudicial Foreclosure Process

Notice to the Trustee

When it becomes clear that lenders, in spite of their helpful efforts on behalf of borrowers, must indeed foreclose, the lenders notify their trustee to begin the process. The trustee could be an individual, corporation, or a partnership. Whoever the trustee is, he or she is part of a three-part trust deed association of beneficiary (lender), trustor (borrower), and trustee (custodian of title).

The trustee will compute all the charges due, including his or her own fees, do some preliminary paperwork, and then prepare the "notice of default."

Filing the Notice of Default

The trustee will record the notice of default in the county in which the property is located. With the county recording, an announcement is made to the public, "This loan's in trouble!" At the same time, the homeowners (trustors) receive a copy of the notice, usually via registered mail.

In bold type, the notice states to the homeowners: "Your loan is in default. Unless the delinquent payments are paid up in cash, in full, your property will be sold without a court action." The notice includes the following information:

1. The date the notice was filed

2. The amount in default; back payments, late fees and trustee charges

3. The principal balance of the loan and its bank identification number

4. The name and phone number of the trustee

5. The name of the lender bringing the action

6. The legal description of the property

7. The names of the parties in default

8. The address of the property

Reinstatement Period

The notice also informs the homeowners about the number of days they have in which to "cure" the default—that is, pay up all that's due in cash. That time span, called the *reinstatement* or *redemption period,* is 106 days long in California and as little as 35 days in some other states. The period starts from the date the notice was recorded.

If the owners manage somehow to pay off the lenders with the proceeds of a new loan, either as the result of a sale or a refinance, a *deed of reconveyance* is recorded by the trustee and the foreclosure action ceases. Or, if the owners make up all the past due payments, late fees, and trustee charges, a *notice of recision* will be recorded by the trustee, canceling the notice of default.

When to Buy Your Distressed Property

It's during the reinstatement or redemption period that you should attempt to work out your deal with the owners in default. Use the following procedure to streamline the process.

Step 1. Do a Market Survey

Order a property profile and comps. Talk with real estate agents to find out what your prospective distressed property, all fixed up, will sell for. Attend "open houses" and compare your probable purchase to your competition. Determine your future net sale price by deducting the costs of sale from the gross sale price. Remember, you must purchase your model for at least 15 percent—preferably 20 percent—below the net sale price.

Step 2. Contact the Owners

In your initial contact—whether by phone, letter, or "cold call"—you must immediately give the owners confidence in you. That's not going to be easy. Why? Because they're suspicious of your motives. By the time you get to them they may have already been approached by the "four exploiters"—attorneys, real estate agents, loan sharks, and investment groups—all wanting to profit from the owners' misfortune. You, by your attitude and demeanor, must convince them that you are the exception. Here's how I suggest you counter the promises of the four exploiters:

Attorneys

Attorneys will try to sell homeowners on the benefits of declaring bankruptcy. You counter that bankruptcy will not extinguish the mortgage lien and will only temporarily halt the foreclosure. It will also have a negative effect on their future employment possibilities and damage their credit rating for a long time. Bankruptcy is expensive both monetarily and emotionally.

Real Estate Agents

There are some insensitive real estate agents out there. They'll try to sweet-talk the hapless owners into giving them a "desperation" listing. You counter that with a real estate agent's sign, open houses, and frequent showings, the whole neighborhood will become aware of the homeowners' plight. In the meantime, their reinstatement period may elapse without a brokered sale. If they were lucky and a brokered sale did take place, the commission would seriously erode any equity they may have.

Loan Sharks

High-interest lenders will tempt the homeowners with "bailout" loans featuring a short term, a high interest rate, and excessive points. You counter that such ripoff schemes merely postpone the foreclosure—they do not cure it. If the homeowners are having trouble with their current payments, they'll most likely have trouble with the newer ones as well.

Investment Groups

The investment groups make promises they rarely can keep, because it takes only one member's dissention to blow up the whole deal. You counter that you're a private investor making your own decisions. You don't have to get "committee" approval.

Finally, the homeowners may say, "My family (friend, partner, and so on) will lend me the money. Explain:

If they wait for those people to come forward—a miracle—they may run out of reinstatement time.

After you've handled the four exploiters, explain your local foreclosure law to the homeowners: the reinstatement period, the trustee sale, and the effect of foreclosure on their credit rating.

Try to ease the homeowners' anger by sympathizing with them. After all, they're going through a terrible turmoil. They may be well aware of the ads in the paper that read, "Attend a free seminar on how to profit from foreclosures." You can be sure they thoroughly resent being the main players in that forum.

Now, during the first encounter, assuming you were able to convince the owners of your honorable intentions, you have to move to the next step in the process:

Step 3. Gather Information and Inspect the Property

Finally, make your pitch: "I'd like to buy this property from you, but first I have to look it over and then ask you for some information."

Have them escort you around the property. Note all the improvements needed—inside and out. When the "tour" is over, sit down and ask for the following information:

1. Loans: Copy down the loan number, monthly payment, interest rate, date due, the lender's name and address, and the loan balance.

2. Determine how many payments are in arrears. Later, contact the lender and tell the loan officer that you're attempting to buy the property and bring everything current. Will the loan officer let you assume the loan? (Chances are good he or she will.)

3. Find out whether the owners have an escrow account to which they've been making monthly payments for taxes and insurance. As part of your deal, you'll want that account transferred to you at no cost.

4. Ask the owners whether there are any other claims on the property—mechanics' liens, IRS liens, and so on.

5. Ask to see their homeowner's insurance policy. Copy down the name of the insurer and policy number, as well as the agent's name, address, and phone number.

Now you're prepared to make a mental assessment as to whether you want to pursue this deal. If the liens revealed by the owners, along with the sums listed on the notice of default, equal or exceed the value of the house compared to the comps you compiled, forget it and move on to another deal.

If that's not the case, you're ready for the next step. But first, make another appointment for about four days later. You need that time to do the following: Check out the liens against the property, determine the cost of rehabilitation, prepare a worksheet, determine the seller's equity, calculate your projected cost of the property, determine your projected profit, and compute the rate of return on your investment.

Step 4. Check Out the Liens Against the Property

You'll want to verify the information about outstanding debts given to you in Step 3 by the owners:

1. Compare what the owners told you in reference to the liens to what you found out from the title company.

2. Call the county tax collector's office to find out whether there are any unpaid real estate taxes.

Step 5. Determine the Cost of Rehabilitation

In the interim between your first and second visits, determine which improvements you're going to have to do to bring the property up to a value that equals or exceeds that of the comps.

Call construction people and get estimates. You'll use them in Step 6.

Step 6. Prepare a Worksheet

Complete the following short worksheet to determine whether you can profit from the deal:

Section A: Cash outlay

1. Amount due on default notice

2. Payments in arrears on first trust deed since the recording of the default notice

3. Payments in arrears on second trust deed

4. Real estate taxes in arrears

    Total cash needed to bring everything current $ _ _ _ _ _ _ _ _

Section B:

5. Principal balance of first trust deed

6. Principal balance of second trust deed

    Total loan amount outstanding $ _ _ _ _ _ _ _ _

Section C:

    Projected costs of improvements to
prepare the property for sale $ _ _ _ _ _ _ _

Section D:

    Holding period costs from acquisition
to sale (approximately 4 months) $ _ _ _ _ _ _ _

Section E:

    Total of A, B, C, and D $ _ _ _ _ _ _ _

This is your projected cost of the project less the owner's equity. That's the next number you must uncover.

Your comps of the area showed what a similar house in good repair would sell for.

Now, your next hurdle is to arrive at a mutually acceptable purchase price to present to the owners—one that may or may not include an equity payment.

Step 7. Determine the Seller's Equity

From the average comp figures, deduct the cost of repairs you determined from construction people's bids that you'll have to make. That number is the "as-is" sale price. In other words, that's the price the owners will have to sell for, because they don't have the money to make the improvements. From that "as-is" sale price, you must also deduct the following in order to arrive at the sellers' equity (in other words, what they would end up with after a sale by a broker):

- Real estate commission, 6 percent

- Approximately four or five months of additional payments before they sell and close escrow

- Escrow, title, and other closing costs

- The balance of the current loan

- The delinquencies on their notice of default

The balance of the "as-is" sale price is the sellers' equity. Very often, it ends up "zero."

Step 8. Determine Your Projected Purchase Price of the Property

Assuming the sellers ultimately will agree to the value of their equity according to your calculations, you must now determine your projected purchase price. Total the following (referring to your worksheet):

- The amount of the loan you'll be assuming, plus any other liens, such as delinquent property taxes

- The total payment of all delinquencies as given in the notice of default

- The sellers' equity

The total of those three numbers equals your projected purchase price.

Step 9. Determine Your Projected Profit

Now you're ready to determine your projected profit. Use the following as a worksheet:

$	Your projected sale price
−	Cost of improvements
−	Cost of holding
−	Purchase price (from Step 8)
$	Net before cost of sale
−	Real estate commission*
−	Escrow and title fees
$	Net profit after sale

*Real estate commission may not apply. It may be best for you to use an "open listing" agreement, which enables you to sell your property yourself and pay no commission; or, in the event you accept a deal brought to you by a real estate agent, you can negotiate a commission with him or her based on the price offered. Open listings do not normally appear in MLS books, however.

Step 10. Compute the Rate of Return

Now calculate the project's rate of return, which is the percentage of profit on the cash you invest.

Cash invested:

$	Cost of paying off delinquencies
+	Rehabilitation expenses
+	Seller's equity
+	Holding costs from acquisition to sale
$	Total cash invested

Now calculate your actual rate from the results of the two previous computations by using this simple equation:

Net profit after sale (step 9) ÷ Total cash invested (step 10) = Rate of return

Remember, to change the decimal result to a percent, you must move the decimal point two places to the right.

I always looked for a rate of return of 50 percent or better. Most of the time I exceeded 75 percent. But you'll decide for yourself what you'll shoot for. Maybe to get your feet wet you could settle for a smaller return and elevate your expectations as you gain experience. At any rate, now you're fully armed to meet your sellers at your second appointment.

Step 11. Meet with Owners a Second Time

Approximately four days later, hold your second appointment with the foreclosure victims.

Present these facts to the owners:

1. Show them the comp sales prices.

2. Show them your calculations from Step 7, indicating their net equity after a brokered "as-is" sale.

3. Offer to pay them the equity indicated at the close of escrow.

4. If they accept your offer and you're satisfied with the deal, have them sign a purchase contract as prescribed by the foreclosure laws in your state.

In California, the sellers have the right to rescind the purchase contract within five days after signing it. Only at the expiration of the period of recision can escrow be opened.

At the point of going to escrow, you must follow the procedures prescribed by your state. In California, the sellers actually sign and record a grant deed that deeds the property to the buyer before escrow closes. But there's a limiting instruction in escrow that says:

> As consideration for the signing and recording of the Grant Deed from sellers to buyers, and immediately after both parties sign these instructions, the buyer agrees to deposit $_____ with the escrow company.
>
> From that amount, with the exception of the trust deeds totaling $_____, the escrow holder is instructed to pay all other outstanding liens, bonds, judgments, foreclosure fees, and encumbrances up to the date of the close of escrow.

Step 12. Carry Out Escrow Instructions

Here are some general escrow instructions that I've used. I present them here for you to add to the purchase contract for your protection:

1. This purchase is contingent on the buyer assuming the existing first trust deed.

2. This purchase is contingent on the buyer's approval of the preliminary title report and its covenants, conditions, and restrictions.

3. Any impound accounts shall be transferred to the owner at no charge.

4. No funds are to be dispersed from escrow until the buyer gives permission.

5. The buyer is to pay all escrow charges.

6. In the event the preliminary title report and outstanding liens are not as previously stated, the buyer has the option to rescind this purchase and recover any money deposited in escrow.

7. Any funds due the sellers will be paid from escrow after they vacate the property.

I make it a practice never to rent the property back to the foreclosed owners.

The process for acquiring a foreclosed property may seem a bit involved. However, you'll be surprised how easily everything will fall into place after you've gone through it a few times. For me, it has been a profitable way to make money in distressed real estate.

The final event facing owners whose property was not purchased during the reinstatement period is the trustee sale.

Trustee Sale: The Final Act in the Process

The trustee sale, which I explain in Chapter 9, is the event in which the property is put up for sale by the trustee and is either purchased by someone for all cash or is taken over by the lender as an REO (real estate owned by lender). The time span for the trustee sale is very short—just five days in California, for instance. By the time the process reaches that point, the foreclosure action is in conclusion and the hapless owners are resigned to the fact that they'll be losing their property.

Deed in Lieu of Foreclosure

Some states have an escape route from foreclosure called a *deed in lieu of foreclosure*. In California, this amounts to the act of the owners in default deeding the property back to the lienholder to avert the time-consuming foreclosure process.

It benefits the homeowners, in that they avoid the stigma of foreclosure, and it saves the lienholder the trouble of a lengthy foreclosure action.

This procedure may not be acceptable to some institutional lenders. They may not accept the deed in lieu and continue to pursue foreclosure. Anyone attempting to use this maneuver should consult a real estate attorney.

A little cash can go a long way.

In Chapter 9, I explain how an investor flushed with cash and facing a trustee sale situation would be more prudent to purchase the defaulted senior lender's loan rather than the property that secures it.

That scenario can also play if you have only a small amount of cash. Here's how.

In your pursuit of foreclosures, make sure you know who's doing the foreclosing. If it turns out that the action is being carried out by a junior lender, you may be onto a good money-making opportunity. In many cases, the junior lender is the former owner who carried back a small $4,000 to $5,000 second or third trust deed when the property was sold to the current owners.

For instance, let's say a house sold for $100,000 and the seller accepted a $20,000 down payment, the buyer took out a new $75,000 loan, and the seller took back the remaining $5,000 of the sale price in a second trust deed. Sometime later, for whatever reason, the buyer stopped making the payments on both the first and second trust deeds, forcing a foreclosure action.

As explained previously, if the action was begun by the holder of the first trust deed, an uninformed junior lender—someone holding a second or third trust deed—could have his or her interest in the property wiped out via a trustee sale. Remember: All trust deeds recorded after the one whose lender is doing the foreclosing can be erased with a trustee sale.

But, in our example, let's assume our seller was not uninformed. This seller was smart and recorded a *request for notice* with the county. That simple document instructed the county recorder to notify the seller in the event that the buyer defaulted on the new $75,000 loan. With that knowledge, our junior lienholder (that is, the seller) would be able to take defensive action.

In order to protect his $5,000 interest in the property, the junior lienholder would have to make the monthly payments to the senior lienholder and pursue a separate foreclosure action. But that could pose a serious cash-flow problem for the seller, who may not have the money with which to make those payments.

The solution to this dilemma would be for you to come in and purchase the seller's second trust deed at a reasonable discount. Then you, the rescuing investor, will assume making payments to the senior lender and pursue your own foreclosure. However, before you assume anything, obtain records about the property's title.

Always do a title search before you invest.

This warning is well taken. You want to be sure of how much money is owed on the property. In some cases I've experienced, properties were subject to mechanics' liens and IRS liens that pushed the claims against the property to a level greater than its market value. So you're wise to be careful.

Special Problems: FHA and VA Foreclosures

U.S. Department of Housing and Urban Development (HUD) affiliate lenders with loans in default have an edge over conventional lenders facing the same situation. The government will pay off their affiliates, thereby relieving them of the responsibility for foreclosure. Conventional lenders don't have a Santa Claus.

When the loan transfer to the government begins, the defaulting borrower will deal directly with HUD—a huge bureaucracy with a tremendous backlog of properties in default.

Rather than taking three or four months for a foreclosure as a conventional lender does, HUD takes a year—sometimes more. In the meantime, the defaultees are living rent free in the house as months of unmade payments accumulate.

The reason HUD takes so long to foreclose partly rests with the fact that the borrowers may ask for and receive a delay in the process if they have a legitimate cause. That delay, along with the traditional government red tape, accounts for the lengthy time lapse.

With a VA project I looked into, the owners were in default for 18 months and still living on the property! I couldn't work a deal with them, because the total of the 18 overdue payments, the lender's late fees, the unpaid property taxes and the loan balance was more than the property's market value.

It's certainly worth a try to pursue a HUD-affiliated foreclosure, but because of the time allowed to elapse, you'll find it difficult to buy HUD foreclosure properties at enough discount to warrant acquiring them as investment real estate.

The purchase of properties in foreclosure provides a continuous source of wealth-building opportunities. Take advantage and take the initiative. While you're helping others, you'll be helping yourself.

Buying Real Estate at Wholesale Prices

REOs

You can search high and low, far and wide for bargain real estate, but I believe the best source is found right in your own local bank and S&L. The source is called REOs—real estate owned by lenders.

How Do REOs Happen?

An REO is the aftermath of a formal foreclosure action. When the lender files a notice of default initiating that process, the homeowners have a lawfully prescribed number of days—the *reinstatement period*—in which to redeem their property and bring the action to a close. However, they can do that only if they can garner enough cash to pay all the past due payments, foreclosure fees, and any other expense demanded in the notice of default.

Here are the homeowners' problems:

1. They have no cash. If they did, they wouldn't be in foreclosure in the first place. Therefore, they cannot meet the demands of the notice of default.

2. Because of their impending poor credit, the homeowners will not be able to qualify to conventionally refinance the property and pay off the defaulted lender with the proceeds of a new loan.

3. With the current over-inventoried housing market, the homeowner very likely will not be able to sell in time to meet the reinstatement period deadline.

4. Furthermore, in most foreclosure situations, a sale usually will not fetch enough cash to pay off all the liens, back payments, late penalties, foreclosure fees, escrow charges, and a real estate agent's commission as well.

5. Family members or friends with enough cash to lend the homeowner to clear the notice of default are usually not forthcoming.

After the borrowers fail to redeem their property during the reinstatement period, the foreclosure action moves to the next stage; a *trustee sale,* conducted by the lender-appointed trustee.

What's a Trustee?

The trustee, or custodian of title, is the party who has the authority to sell the property when the borrowers default in their loan payments. However, the sale can take place only at the request of the lender. Hence, the term "trustee sale."

Trustee Sale

After the reinstatement period expires, the property "goes to sale." The sale period, of short duration, is set by the government; in California, it is only five days long.

What the sale period amounts to is a public announcement of a lender's auction. Notices of trustee sales are published in local, metropolitan, and professional newspapers. They're also posted at designated public areas of city hall.

As an investor, you can subscribe to professional information-gathering services that will send you their monthly or bimonthly listings for a fee. Although not government related, you can get in touch with those companies by asking a clerk at the county recorder's office for the services' phone numbers.

Despite the fact that trustee sales are easily accessible by the public, unfortunately for lenders, few of them are successful; few properties actually sell at the event.

The kicker to trustee sales is that lenders want to be completely paid off. They want all the back payments, late penalties, foreclosure fees, and the balance of the loan—all in cash. That's a pretty tall order and accounts for the small number of purchases.

Sale Procedures

The sale itself is usually conducted by a representative of the trustee. Although it could take place in a title company office or a law firm, the sale is usually held at an easily identifiable and less intimidating site—like the front steps of city hall, for instance.

At the sale, the trustee's representative appears with a handful of trustee sale notices. Then the rep reads off the description and price of the first property being offered for sale that day. At the conclusion of this rapid recitation, the rep asks whether anyone is prepared to purchase the property. If there's a positive response, the rep notes that and then proceeds to the next property on the agenda. If there's no response, the property becomes an REO—a property owned by the lender.

Where the Investor Enters the Negotiations

Publication of the trustee sale is the investor's clue to track a property—but only to find out whether it reverted to the lender if unsold—*not* to pay all cash for it.

Why should you pay all cash for a property at the trustee sale when you may be able to purchase that same property or one like it from the lender for little or no cash?

Pay cash for the loan, not the property.

Now, if you're an investor intent on using a lot of cash, a better deal for you would be to try to purchase the defaulted loan at a substantial discount after the lender files the notice of default. Try any discount, because you never know just how disgusted the lender may be with the whole affair!

After you acquire the note, you can complete the foreclosure yourself. A few things could happen:

- If the homeowners somehow manage to cure the default, they'll have to pay you the original sum listed in the notice of default. Then, they must resume making the loan payments to you according to their original loan agreement.

- If they fail to cure the default, and the property goes to sale, a buyer will have to pay you the full amount of the original loan and the other listed default charges, all in cash.

- If no buyer emerges at the trustee sale, and you end up with the property, you will, in effect, have purchased it at a formidable discount—a nice reward for the large amount of cash you invested.

Of course, after you own the property, you can refinance it and take out all your money.

Do lenders sell their loans in default? Some do; some don't. How do you find out? Simple. You ask.

How to Prepare Yourself to Capitalize on an REO Deal

Follow the steps in this section so you'll be prepared to jump on an attractive REO.

Step 1. Ask Your Bank or S&L Whether Any REOs Are Available

Contact the "real estate owned" division of your local bank or S&L and ask if they have any properties available for sale. If one of the loan officers says yes but puts you in touch with a real estate agent, you'll not be able to cut a good enough deal for yourself. Why? Because the lender, most likely, will have already spent money on repairing the property, and the agent will have it listed at market value. Therefore, go on to Step 2 and find another deal.

But if the lender says an REO is available, and you caught it before the lender spent money on the property, or before the lender put it up for sale with a real estate agent, you're ready for Step 3 and can skip Steps 2 and 4.

Step 2. Track Trustee Sales

If Step 1 doesn't work, track down trustee sale notices. Where do you find them?

- County recorder's office
- Monthly legal listing services
- Neighborhood newspapers
- Metropolitan newspapers
- Professional newspapers

153

Using those sources, locate some distressed, entry-level properties in those areas in which you'd like to invest.

Step 3. Visit the Properties

Make an on-site visit to properties that best fit your criteria: Entry-level housing in a good neighborhood, in need of superficial repairs, surrounded by well-maintained properties. Select the one you want to purchase and note on your calendar the date, time, and place of its trustee sale.

Step 4. Find Out Whether the Lender Owns the Property

If possible, attend the trustee sale to determine first hand whether or not the property was purchased. If you don't have time to attend the sale, call the lender the next business day and ask the "real estate owned" department if they now own it.

Step 5. Make an Appointment to Inspect the Property

As soon as you know the lender owns the property, tell the loan officer you'd like to place a bid to buy it but would like to inspect it first.

Make an appointment with him or her to do so as soon as possible. Make sure you ask the lender whether the institution will finance your purchase. Most of the time it will. But, if the lender won't make a loan to you, before going any further, you should make some preliminary financial arrangements with another lender.

Step 6. Inspect the Property and Note the Needed Repairs

With the bank's rep accompanying you, inspect the property. Note all the improvements you'll have to make inside and out in order to put the property in top condition for sale. Tell the lender's rep you'll have a bid ready at the latest, the next day.

If this sounds urgent, it's for a reason. You have to beat your competitors to the bargaining table.

Step 7. Do a Market Survey

After your inspection and while you're still in the neighborhood, do a market survey of comparable properties.

Look for properties similar to your prospective purchase but in tip top condition and currently for sale. Note the addresses and real estate agents' phone numbers on those properties.

Pretending you're a buyer, use a local phone booth, call the real estate agents and ask for the list price and amenities of each property. If a real estate agent insists on meeting with you before giving you any information, comply with the request. Don't feel guilty about wasting the agent's time. Remember, if you make your deal, improve the property and then offer it for sale under an open listing agreement. It may be he or she who sells it for you for a handsome commission. Besides, a meeting with a real estate agent can help you. How?

- You'll have the chance to closely inspect a property that may be your competition.

- You can ask the real estate agent what the sale prices have been for this type of property. Remember, the list price is not the sale price.

If the real estate agent will not divulge the actual going sale prices, you can arbitrarily deduct 10 to 15 percent off the list price to arrive at a probable number.

Step 8. Determine Your Net Sale Price

You must know your net sale price before you make a bid to buy the property. If, for instance, you find out that your property, all fixed up, will sell for $150,000, the net from the sale will be something like this:

$	150,000	Sale price
−	9,000	6% real estate agent's commission
	141,000	Adjusted sale price
−	1,500	Approximately 1% of the sale price for escrow and other fees
$	139,500	Net sale price to seller

155

Step 9. Determine Your Highest Offer and Work Within Limits

Your bid *must* be 15 to 20 percent lower than the $139,500 net sale price.

$	139,500	Net sale price
×	.20	Discount percentage
	27,900	Discount
$	111,600	Target bid price

Besides purchasing the property at or near the $111,600 mark, if you work within the following limits (described in detail in earlier chapters), you'll stand a good chance of making 50 percent or more profit on all your cash invested:

1. Put 10 percent or less down.

2. Pay no loan points to the lender. (This is usually not a problem. Lenders, so eager to divest themselves of REOs, will not let loan points stand in the way of a sale.)

3. Limit your repair expenditures to about 5 percent of your projected sale price.

4. Hold the property for under six months from acquisition to sale or rent.

Step 10. Estimate the Cost of Repairs

Try not to exceed 5 percent of the sale price of $150,000. Call merchants and tradespeople for estimates. Don't begin any work until you own the property.

Step 11. Predetermine Your Future Net Profit

Here's the calculation that reveals what your net profit will be:

$	111,600	Attempted purchase price from the lender
−	11,600	Approximate down payment of 10%
$	100,000	Note taken back by lender at 9.5% for 30 years. Payments will be $841 per month.

Cash Expended

$	11,600	Down payment
+	4,205	Five payments from acquisition to sale (5 × $841)
+	7,500	Approximate costs of improvements: 5% of sale price of $150,000
$	23,305	Total cash invested

Sale Proceeds Five Months After Purchase

$	150,000	Your sale price
–	4,500	3% real estate agent's commission using an open listing
–	1,500	Approximately 1% of sale price for escrow and other fees
	144,000	Your net sale price
–	100,000	First trust deed taken back by lender
	44,000	Net cash from sale
–	23,305	Cash invested
$	20,695	Profit of almost 90% on cash invested

Knowing your possible profit on a deal like this will sharpen your negotiating skills and provide you with the knowledge about how far up your purchase offer can rise.

Step 12. Ask for the Moon When You Negotiate with the Lender

Follow these tips in your negotiations:

1. Start with a purchase price offer of $105,000.

2. Start with zero down.

3. Offer to buy the property "as is." Lenders like that.

4. Offer a fast escrow—10 days or less. Lenders like that, too!

5. Ask the lender to carry back the purchase price in a loan at the best current terms and charge no points.

157

6. Ask the lender to add the cost of the repairs to the loan. Offer to put those funds in an escrow account with their withdrawal authorized only as repairs are completed.

Now, you're not likely to get all of these terms. But, that's what you could start with. The more negotiating planks in your verbal offer, the better you can trade off and compromise.

Offer the lender two deal "sweeteners":

- A nonrefundable earnest money deposit. That will ensure him that you're serious and will consummate the purchase. Defaulted lenders like to know that if they enter into a sale contract with you, they'll have a "done" deal.

- You'll purchase the property with no contingencies except a clear title report.

In Step 11, you saw a potential profit of about 90 percent on all the invested cash. If you'd feel comfortable with less than that, you could afford to purchase for a higher price, if the bank demands it.

It has been my experience that you can buy an REO for as little as 15 percent under the projected net sale price and still do very well. The price you pay the lender will depend on your competition, the lender's REO inventory, and the intensity of his desire to unload the property.

However, if the lender insists on a price that prohibits your making at least a 50 percent profit on all sums invested, look for another deal.

Step 13. Sign Your Written Offer and Go to Escrow

In making your final bid to lock the lender into the deal, remember to overstate the extent of the property's deterioration and the costs of repairs. Your lender, after listening to your proposals, will say something like this, "We have to receive X number of dollars from the sale to cover our losses." If your offer and the lender's bottom line are reasonably close, you'll have a deal.

With the price settled, go to escrow as soon as possible. You want to close out any competitors who may be waiting in the wings.

Where do you get the down payment money for the deal? If you can't make a zero-down deal with the lender, use some of the sources described in Chapter 4, "Scratching Up Your First Down Payment." If no one source covers your capital needs, try a combination of the sources listed there.

How about the money needed for holding and improvements—where does that come from?

Assuming the lender may not take you up on your request for adding the cost of the repairs to your loan, you can try some of the same sources listed in Chapter 4. However, remember the Title I program explained in Chapter 7? Lenders making those loans will advance you up to $17,500 for home improvements. That's an excellent source of repair money, and you can get that loan within three weeks after you own the property. Keep in mind that that's not an "equity-based" loan. Because the lender is guaranteed payment by the Federal Housing Authority (FHA), the lender only looks to your creditworthiness and the sufficiency of your income to qualify you for it.

This chapter outlined a method I've used to purchase REOs. Now, it's up to you. Try it. If you're persistent, you'll find your first deal and profit handsomely from it. Why not start right now? Your future depends on what you do now. Dream of a better life—fantasize a world of opulence. Then do what it takes to make it all come true.

Auctions: Your Tool for Selling and Buying Properties

Mention the word *auction* and immediately the idea of "desperation" comes to the minds of many people. They tend to think that any seller using an auction to sell off real estate or other assets is in some state of emergency. Nonsense! Although that may have been a valid assumption years ago, today it is no longer true. Now, the auction is used as the marketing vehicle of choice by vendors of a large variety of products—everything from cattle, grain, and priceless art to single family homes, condos, and shopping centers.

Especially in a slow market, the auction has become a primary selling method for some developers of large housing projects. Because their costs of holding inventory awaiting conventional sales has become extremely expensive, the fast, economical auction is a financial and marketing godsend for them—and for investors too! Stories are now surfacing about the bargains some buyers are picking up at new tract auctions—houses and condos at 20 to 30 percent below market value. For people who have done their pre-auction homework and lined up good financing as well, the "new product" auction is a windfall of good luck. Although I usually advocate buying distressed properties, the purchase of newly constructed housing at 20 to 30 percent below market is another wonderful way to accumulate wealth. The idea is especially good if the tract auctioneer has in-house lenders giving below-market interest rates on loans to successful bidders.

How to Use the Auction to Sell Your Property

For the entrepreneur, the slower paced the market is, the higher the premium for turning standing inventory into liquid cash. Can you see how, for instance, if you had a fast auction sale on a property in a buyer's market, you'd then be able to go out and make a couple of bargain purchases to boost your net worth? *Fast* and *economical* are the two adjectives that best describe the sale auction. But to achieve a speedy, money-saving sale, the auctioneer must do some marketing chores weeks in advance of the auction date.

Auctioneer's Preauction Marketing Activities

Any of the following activities could, and sometimes do, produce an offer and sale even before the auction takes place:

1. Illustrated brochures are prepared and sent out to targeted customers selected from lists of thousands of potential buyers.

2. Descriptive ads are prominently placed in carefully chosen newspapers announcing the property's preauction viewing dates, the auction date, the certified deposit check required, and the minimum bid, if there is one.

3. Cooperating brokers and sales agents are notified in advance so that they can prepare bids to submit for their clients.

The scope of the auctioneer's preauction marketing activity depends on the motivation of the sellers. How urgent is the sale to them? That really translates to: How much can they afford to spend on advertising? It's the sellers, after all, who will foot the main portion of that bill, which could range anywhere from a few hundred to thousands of dollars. Most auctioneers require the sellers to pay their portion of the marketing expenses up front.

However, sellers may find it more profitable to trade the four- or five-month holding period usually necessary in a conventional sale for the advertising expense of a five- or six-week auction process.

Besides advertising expenses, the property owners pay a commission to the auctioneer who must, in many states, be licensed to sell real estate. The amount of commission is usually negotiable, is payable only if there is a successful sale, and is normally deducted from the seller's sale proceeds.

Three Major Types of Auctions

Not all auctions are the same. Following is a description of the three most popular types.

Absolute Auction

In this type of auction, the owners agree to sell the property to the highest bidder—period! They don't require nor do they post a minimum sale price. Because of the bidding freedom given here, this is sometimes referred to as an auction "without reserve" and as such, it attracts the greatest number of bidders. With such a large, competing pool of potential buyers, it may be the best way to get the highest price.

Absolute Minimum Auction

In this type of auction, the sellers post the minimum amount they'll accept for the property. The bidding must reach or exceed this posted minimum or no sale will take place. If the auction itself doesn't produce a sale at the minimum price, the sellers, sometimes with the auctioneer acting as their agent, can attempt to strike a deal with the highest bidder after the auction is over.

163

Reserve Auction

As with the absolute auction, there's no minimum price posted in the reserve auction. However, it differs from the absolute auction in that rather than having to accept the highest bid, the sellers retain the right to refuse it if they deem it unacceptable.

Although a "sale" at an auction can decrease your holding period and possibly increase your profits on a project, a "no-auction sale" can open your eyes to certain realities—provided the auctioneer upheld his or her end of the deal and managed the auction properly. Reasons for a no-auction sale include these:

- Your sale price expectation may have been set too high.

- Economic conditions weren't right—too many properties for sale, for instance.

In the event of a no-auction sale, rather than conventionally remarketing the property, it may be a better idea to rent it out for a while and wait for a more favorable selling climate.

What Makes an Auction "Sell?"

Following are features of auctions that make them an attractive means of selling your formerly distressed properties:

- The electricity in the room stimulates in the bidders an "urgent desire" to buy, to out-bid the competition.

- There's no conflict between the buyer and seller. The bidder alone makes his or her own uncompromised decisions.

- Competition reigns supreme.

- The seller, to fulfill the desire for a sale on a given date by a certain time, will, more likely, be motivated to set a realistic price.

- The people present at an auction are ready, willing, and able prospective buyers—there are no "looky loos."

- One excited bidder can generate a sense of urgency in the other bidders and can boost the price up significantly.

- The sale price is established by a room full of bidders—not just one buyer.

- As the seller, you can make an on-the-spot decision to accept or reject a bid.

- Because the successful bidder must submit a cashier's check and, in many instances, sign a liquidating damages clause wherein he or she agrees to lose the deposit if he or she fails to complete the sale, the bidder will do everything necessary to achieve a successful escrow closing.

- All sales activity is condensed into one area and in one time period.

Remember: Before you choose an auction company, attend at least two of its events to witness how well attended they are, how professionally they are conducted, and how well their deals are consummated.

Make sure you get a marketing agenda and a briefing as to how the auctioning firm will advertise your property. Know all costs up front. Determine which of the three types of auctions you'll use and keep in mind: The auction is not always a guaranteed sale.

How to Use the Auction to Buy a Distressed Property

If you mentally prepare yourself for the fact that you're going to go to an auction and you're going to actually acquire the property up for bid, you'll do all the necessary investigative research beforehand, as if you were buying from a lender or private party. Leave nothing out!

Preauction Research

Follow these steps to prepare yourself for an auction purchase:

1. Visit the area of the property. Make sure it's in a neighborhood in which you'd like to invest.

2. Get sales comps from local real estate agents and a title company.

3. Get a property profile or a title report.

4. Know what your future net sale price will be after your rehab. (The net sale price is the gross sale price less the normal expenses of sale.)

5. Deduct 15 to 20 percent from that number; that's your highest bid figure, although you'll begin your bidding much lower than that.

6. Know whether there's a minimum bid required. It might amount to more than your highest bid figure, therefore making it useless for you to attend the auction.

7. Review the property on its open-house dates and carefully determine everything that must be done to bring it up to an ideal sale condition.

8. Determine the costs of doing the rehab.

9. If repairs will cost more than 5 percent of your future sale price, lower your "highest bid" figure.

10. Know how you'll finance the purchase. It's best to prequal-ify for your loan. There's no point in bidding on property if you're unsure of the source of your money. If you don't have your lender in place and you're the highest bidder, you may lose your certified deposit check if you fail to complete the purchase.

11. Have your certified check in the designated amount ready. You'll not be allowed to bid without it.

Do all 11 steps whether you intend to sell or rent the property. Be particularly careful in compiling your comps. I've been to auctions where the bidding got so heated that the price paid far exceeded the property's true market value as evidenced by recent sales comps. The successful bidder apparently had no idea of the area's house values. Especially in a slowly appreciating market, that's a terrible mistake to make!

---

*If you load your brain with knowledge,
you'll line your pockets with money.
Practical knowledge creates wealth.*

There are auctions for everything, held everywhere, for many different reasons. Although real estate is a relative newcomer to the auction block, I predict you'll be seeing more and more in the future.

Where to Look for Advertised Auctions

Here are some primary sources of auction announcements:

- Professional journals
- Notices in local newspapers
- Real estate sections of your Sunday paper
- Business section of your daily paper

Contact local auctioneers to add your name to their mailing lists and receive descriptive property brochures well in advance of the auction dates.

Also check the bulletin boards at your county court house and city hall. Make it a point to subscribe to firms who publish monthly marketing lists of probate sales, foreclosures, and bankruptcies.

Occasions for Auctions

Following are some common events that prompt auctions of property:

- *Foreclosures:* The trustee sale—final act of the foreclosure process. See Chapter 8.

- *Probate:* Disposal of a deceased person's property. It's probably not a good source for entrepreneurial discount housing seekers, because the property must be sold for at least 90 percent of its appraised value. That's not enough of a discount for an investor unless the appraisal comes in very low. A judge must approve the sale price at the confirmation hearing. During the confirmation hearing, someone can come in and overbid you, negating all the preparation time you invested.

- *Bankruptcy:* Contact law firms who act as trustees in bankruptcy and ask to be placed on their mailing list.

- *IRS Tax Sale:* Property that the IRS confiscates is sold to pay back taxes. See Chapter 3.

- *Sheriff's Sale:* Assets seized by the court with the intent to sell in order to satisfy a judgment against a defendant. Notices are posted at the county court house; or call the sheriff's office—staff may have a mailing list.

- *County Tax Lien Sales:* In many counties, if an owner gets five years behind in the payment of real estate taxes, the property will be seized by the tax collector and auctioned off to the highest bidder. The tax sales usually take place every three months or so. If the county tax collector's office has a mailing list, call to add your name to it. If there is no mailing list, call intermittently and ask when the next auction will take place.

Before you bid at an auction sponsored by the IRS, sheriff's office, or county, attend a few as an observer. That will give you a good idea about whether you'll be able to buy at a big enough discount.

Now, let's set the stage for an actual auction.

The Auction Scene

You pull up to the auction site, a distressed three-bedroom, single-family home in a modest, well-kept neighborhood. Getting there about 30 minutes ahead of time, you figure you'll be able to find a parking space, register, and give the property a final walk-through.

Although you arrived early, you're surprised to see a score of people already there, milling about the front lawn, clutching their bidding numbers.

After parking the car about a block and a half away, you approach the property and notice the range of people present—young, old, obviously prosperous, and obviously not—and you wonder how many of these people are bidders and how many are merely observers? Judging by the large number of visible bidding cards, you become a little uptight and conclude you'll probably be facing a real contest here! On the front lawn, a small platform and microphone are set up. The auctioneers, seated nearby at a portable table, are busy registering the prospective bidders, making sure they each have their proper certified check ready, and assigning them a bidding number. You stand in line and patiently wait your turn.

When the appointed hour arrives, the auctioneer steps up to the mike and gives you a little pitch about the property, pointing out its amenities and quoting recent sale prices in the area. If there's a minimum bid required, he or she will announce it at this point.

With that out of the way, the crowd settles down and the auctioneer pounds the gavel. "Do I have a bid for $100,000?" The auction has begun.

Auction Strategy

There are certain strategies that you'll develop as you attend auctions. First, though, let me point out the presence of "shills." They're usually present to stimulate bidding but actually buy nothing.

Don't make an on-the-spot decision to bid higher than your predetermined price. That's how you play into the hands of the shills, overpay for the property, and ultimately lose money.

Make an opening bid *only* if you have the guts to bid very low. After anyone's opening bid, the auctioneer will try to keep upping the bidding in large increments, from a $100,000 bid received, to a $110,000 bid asked, for instance. When that happens don't be afraid to offer an incremental bid of, say, $102,000. It may slow the pace of the bidding down somewhat and may keep the price from escalating out of hand.

If the property doesn't sell during the bidding, try to make a deal with the auctioneer after the auction. It's done often, and you may make a good buy.

A major difference between a conventional sale and an auction is this: In a conventional sale, you start with a list price and negotiate downward; in an auction, you start with a minimum price and bid upward. The results in both cases are the same—sale at market value or below.

You can use an auction as a seller and as a buyer by carefully doing your homework and by never deviating from the basic principles that guarantee your profits.

Condos and Co-ops as Investments

Given today's prices for houses, even for fixer-uppers, many first-time investors find they can't come up with sufficient capital to enter that lucrative market. Because of their lower costs, condos and co-ops have become an especially attractive alternative for first-time investors. However, before you weigh whether to invest in a future income-producing condo or co-op, you have to check one important detail: Does the homeowners association of your selected building permit rentals? Some do not; they demand all their units be owner-occupied. You must be particularly careful about your ability to rent when you deal with co-ops. I'll get to that in a moment.

First, here are definitions of a condo and a co-op. A condo is a housing unit in which ownership consists of air-space inside the walls of an apartment and an undivided interest in the building's recreation facilities and land. You have control over the air-space of your apartment and can decorate as you wish, but anything you may want to do that alters the exterior appearance of the unit must be approved by the elected officers of the homeowners association. A co-op is a housing unit in which ownership consists of a share of stock in the corporation that owns the building. Along with the share of stock comes a proprietary lease on a particular unit in the complex.

Whereas in a condo you have an *ownership* interest in the building evidenced by a deed to a particular unit, in a co-op, your proprietary interest is evidenced by a *share of stock* in the corporation. Although you don't "own" your unit, you do have the right to use it as you wish, within the confines of your lease and homeowner regulations. Each stockholder makes a monthly payment to the homeowners association commensurate to his proportionate square footage share of the building. Traditionally, co-ops have been more restrictive in their tenancy requirements than condos.

Board of Directors

The board of directors of many co-op buildings can wield a great deal of power. For instance, the board can pass judgment on who will and who will not reside in the building. If the board feels that the presence of a certain family or individual will threaten the security of their current ownership, they can deny the sale of a unit to that entity. In many co-ops, there exists one mortgage and one real estate tax bill covering the entire building. Both condos and co-ops are governed by an elected board of directors.

The duties and restrictions of the board are outlined in the by-laws of the building.

Always ask for a copy of the by-laws when you purchase a condo or a co-op.

Another document you must have is the current annual report. It will indicate the financial status of the building and will disclose whether the association is operating within its income. Make sure the report discloses that the association is making regular contributions to a reserve fund for the repair or replacement of major common area components such as the roof, elevator, and pool equipment.

If you invest in a co-op or condo in a building where there is evidence of serious deferred maintenance, make sure you're not going to be assessed for corrections that should have been paid for by the seller.

Converted Units

In the 1970s and 1980s many established apartment houses were converted to condos or co-ops. Because they were conversions, they sold for considerably less than newly constructed units. Their entrance on the market partially filled the gap for much-needed lower-income housing. Depending on the developer or convertor, those units, while legally assuming the name condo or co-op, were in reality nicely refurbished apartments. Because of budgetary restraints and structural limitations, some amenities normally included in newly constructed units by necessity had to be eliminated in the converted ones. For example, most newly constructed units have individual laundry rooms and wood-burning fireplaces, but converted units as a rule do not.

Implications for Investors

Converted units will usually rent for less than their newly constructed counterparts, because they often lack some of the amenities found in the constructed units. You may get better results advertising the availability of your converted unit under the apartment for rent heading of your newspaper rather than the condo or co-op for rent section.

173

Converted units do not appreciate as rapidly as newly constructed ones. You're also more apt to have maintenance problems in an older, converted building than in a newly constructed one, making you liable for future assessments.

A plus feature of the converted unit is that it stands a better chance of being in a well-established, well-located neighborhood. You quite possibly will have a lower vacancy problem as a result.

Advantages of Condos and Co-ops as Investments

All condos and co-ops, new and converted, are about the easiest investment properties to own. Because all the exterior maintenance is handled by your homeowner association through the payment of your monthly dues, other than an occasional plumbing problem, the units themselves are practically care-free.

You must make your tenants aware of house rules and regulations. Your rental agreement must state that if they fail to abide by the house rules, they will put their tenancy in jeopardy.

Evaluation Techniques for Condos and Co-ops

Price

Basically, you proceed to price a condo or co-op the same as you would a single family home. First, know what price range you can afford. Then, begin your market research in the neighborhood that matches your pocketbook. Look for an entry-level unit in need of repair located in a well-maintained building. Consult your usual bargain real estate sources—foreclosures and REOs. If nothing is available from those sources, consult real estate agents who have listings in your desired areas. Explain to them what you're after and let them compile a list of possibilities. Real estate brokers belong to multiple listing services that publish all currently available listed properties. Get copies of the properties you're interested in so that you can make comparisons.

Role of the Real Estate Agent

There's one caveat you should know in dealing with a real estate agent. Don't reveal to the agent the highest price you'd be willing to pay for a property. For instance: An agent shows you a property that meets your requirements. You decide to make a bid below the asking price. Don't say, "I really like that property, Mrs. Jones. I'd be willing to pay $100,000 for it, but try to get it for me for $80,000." If your agent is a member of the National Association of Realtors and abides by that organization's rules, she will have to reveal your price range to the listing agent when your offer is presented. Why? Because, with the presentation of your offer, your agent becomes the listing agent's subagent.

Many people don't realize that most agents represent the seller, not the buyer.

It is the seller who pays the agent's commission. The multiple listing services require that when an agent shows a buyer a property, that agent is, in effect, accepting the unilateral offer of the listing agent to act as his or her subagent. Therefore, your agent really will be working for the seller—even though you, the buyer, are the agent's client. Many conscientious agents attempt to develop a good rapport with their buyers. They try to give the outward impression that they are acting solely on their behalf. Be careful. An agent has the responsibility to disclose to the buyers the agent's obligation to the seller. The agent should do that before he or she begins showing the property. However, the revelation of that important detail is often withheld from the buyers.

Buyer's Agent

A growing practice among investors is the employment of a "buyer's agent." A buyer's agent owes no allegiance to the sellers and in fact does not receive any commission from them. The agent may base the sales fee on a percentage of the purchase price or some other mutually agreeable arrangement, and that fee will be paid by the *buyer,* not the sellers.

The buyer and buyer's agent should enter into a formal contract that clearly states the duties of both parties. As the buyer's gesture of fidelity to the agent, the buyer could offer a small advance of the future fee, the remainder of which will be paid after the successful closing of escrow. If a deal that offers a percentage of the listing commission to the selling agent is struck, the buyer's agent will deduct that amount from the agreed on purchase price. Then, at the close of escrow, the buyer will settle with the agent.

There are distinct advantages to having a buyer's agent contract. Having a real estate professional work for you locating properties can save you a lot of mileage and a lot of time. What that agent could do in a few hours could take you weeks to accomplish. Besides having access to the multiple listing service, a real estate agent's constant travelling around makes him or her eminently aware of what's available in the marketplace.

Here's another advantage. A buyer's agent does not have to rely only on real estate agents' multiple listings for available inventory. The agent can access "for sale by owner" properties as well. Remember, a buyer's agent is not getting paid by a seller, you—the purchaser—are paying the fee. He or she can go a step further than the listings everyone knows about. If the type of property you seek is not currently for sale in your market area, a buyer's agent can locate unlisted properties, contact the owners, and offer them a deal. Keep the buyer's agent idea in mind. It's a relationship that could prove fruitful in your search for investments.

In my real estate career, purchase price has always been king. That price has always been based on my knowledge of the future net sale price of the distressed project immediately after refurbishing it. By buying 15 to 20 percent below that future net sale price my profit is built into the deal at the onset. You see, I don't engage in guessing games in business. If you never violate that principle—and I mean *never*—you can't help but get rich in real estate.

Location

Most city planners position apartments, condos, and co-ops in buffer zones sandwiched between commercial centers and enclaves of single family homes. As a rule, that positioning usually means that they are close to shopping centers and major road arteries. That being the case, good location is often a built-in feature of condos and co-ops. I like and invest in condos or co-ops that are within walking distance of minimarkets, hair salons, cleaners, and pharmacies. The nearness of those conveniences deemphasizes the necessity of using an auto for minor shopping trips. It also makes your unit more attractive as a rental or sale to older people who may not be able to drive.

Because they have the reputation of being crime areas, try not to buy into buildings that border on or back up to alleys. If they are located on a street with numerous apartment buildings, extra parking facilities pose a problem for condos and co-ops. Despite the fact that most of those units have the equivalency of two parking spaces, that is usually not enough to accommodate visiting guests, who then must park on the street. Most of the time that parking area is taken up by the second cars of the neighboring apartment house dwellers.

Financing

Condos

The FHA decided to delete all purely investment financing from its portfolio. Officials felt they were getting away from the original intent of the FHA—to provide low-cost financing for individual home buyers. Although funding for two- to four-unit apartment houses is still available, the borrower must agree to live in one of the units in order for the loan to be approved. It is possible to turn an FHA financed condo into a rental. Your original intent, however, must be to purchase the unit as a personal residence. Then, after living there for six months to a year, it's permissible to move out and offer the unit as a rental. Beside the FHA, conventional financing is readily available from many banks and S&Ls. They offer the usual 80 percent loan-to-value financing with 20 percent down.

However, you can try to be a little more creative. If there's assumable financing, you may save the cost of a new loan by taking over the old one. Ask the owners to carry back a second trust deed. That may help reduce your down payment. If the sellers do agree to take back a second trust deed, go one step further. Try to talk them into deferring payments on the loan for a year. That quite possibly would avoid your having a negative cash flow in that crucial first year of operation. Refer to Chapter 6 for more financing ideas.

Keep in mind that there are six major expense items in the operation of a rental condo or co-op:

- homeowner dues

- taxes

- insurance

- repairs

- vacancies

- mortgage payments

Which expense can you directly control? Mortgage payments. Pay a lot of attention to them. You have to live with your decision for a long time. If you buy a distressed unit for 15 to 20 percent under market and get the best possible financing, you will ensure a profitable deal.

Co-ops

Financing co-ops in many states poses a problem. Because the security instrument for a co-op is a share of stock rather than a direct interest in the real estate itself, lenders must devise new operational procedures to handle them. Few have taken the trouble to do so. Those co-ops that do have traditional loans are most likely those whose initial development was financed by a participating lender.

That lender usually imposed one mortgage on the entire building, and individual lessors paid their proportionate share of the monthly payments through the homeowners association.

In Southern California, in order to refinance a co-op, you have to go to sources outside the traditional banks and savings and loans. That means an owner ends up paying higher than normal interest rates—higher than average loan origination fees. On top of that, the owner will have to settle for a loan duration of much less than the traditional 30 years. As a result of this hardship, many Southern California co-ops are seeking state and local approval to convert to condos. Because of the absence of easy financing, unless you live in an area where co-ops are conventionally funded, I do not recommend them as a viable investment vehicle.

Vacancy Factors and Owner Occupancy

There are *two* vacancy factors you have to consider before buying an investment condo or co-op. First, there is the building's vacancy factor which is influenced by the number of owner-occupants. The higher the percentage of owner-occupants in a building, the lower its rental vacancy factor will be and the better your investment. The homeowners association keeps a record of the building's occupants and can tell you the number of owner-occupants. Buildings that are beautifully and impeccably maintained usually indicate a high owner-occupancy rate. Those units enjoy the highest rate of appreciation and the lowest rate of rental vacancy. Be careful. Some condo and co-op complexes have so many rented units in them that they are really more like apartment houses.

After you've determined the building's vacancy rate, you have to consider the vacancy factor of the neighborhood of your prospective purchase. That will take some time and leg work. You have to go to similar buildings in the area and note the number of "for rent" signs visible. Then you have to visit those units in order to make a judicious comparison. Note the amenities of each unit visited. A tell-tale sign of the number of vacancies in a building is the number of mailboxes with no names attached. Because mailboxes are usually pretty accessible, that is one of the first things I note in doing my neighborhood vacancy research. If a locked entrance prevents you from getting to the mailboxes, check the gas meters. They're usually located on the sides or at the front of the building. The meters with tags on them usually indicate the service has been shut off, implying a vacant unit. I learned that technique from a mortgage banker. In the 1970s, when Southern California had a double-digit vacancy factor in many areas, it was difficult for apartment house owners and investors to get financing. Before a lender would commit to a loan, the institution would send someone out to the building to determine the vacant units there. Owners, of course, were onto this and would disguise their vacancies by closing the blinds or draperies of their unoccupied units. That way, when the investigator arrived, he or she could not look inside the unit to determine whether someone was living there. As soon as lenders were aware of the apartment house owners' devious concealment activities, they came up with something else—tagged gas meters. Lenders' reps went out and counted the number of tagged gas meters.

When owners got wind of that, you can be sure, as vacancies occurred, off came those tell-tale gas meter tags. Over a period of time, the vacancy factor in many areas of Southern California tumbled to 5 percent. Financing became plentiful again; the cat and mouse game with lenders' reps was over.

Remember, the higher the vacancy factor, the lower the price of the unit! A reasonable neighborhood's vacancy factor is 5 percent and under. If the rate goes too far above 5 percent, you should bargain the price down. Scan the real estate or business section of your paper for articles on vacancy rates in different areas of your community. Look in the weekend edition of your local paper under "condos for rent." You can get a good idea of the number of units currently available. That's a terrific indication of the vacancy rate of an area.

When you're in the rental business, be prepared for vacancies. They *will* happen—usually at the most inopportune time. You must keep a nest egg of cash to cover three major items of expenses you'll be faced with at that time:

- Three to four months of mortgage payments
- The cost of refurbishing the unit

• Your monthly homeowners association dues

Keep in mind that vacancies are a part of the rental business. If you're financially prepared, they'll pose no major problem. In fact, as you'll find out in Chapter 12 about apartment houses, a vacancy is usually your opportunity to bring your unit's income up to the market rate!

Building and Unit Amenities

Building

The number of amenities in a building is often determined by its overall size and the price range of its units. In huge complexes, everything from a putting green to tennis courts, pools, spas, and fitness centers can be found. However, the first basic building amenity that I have found most in demand by renters and potential buyers is the presence of a security system. It's a sign of our times, but people really appreciate the safe feeling locked gates give them. This is especially true for buildings located right in or close to urban centers.

The second basic building amenity that people look for are parking facilities. Show me a complex with ample parking, and I'll show you a winner. We are an auto-dependent society and demand safe, ample accommodations for our vehicles. In my opinion, those two basic building amenities should be present in every complex, no matter what its size or the price range of its units. Other building amenities such as elevators, provisions for the handicapped, outdoor lighting, and well-maintained gardens are all features that add to a unit's value. In your market comparisons, you can trade one amenity for another as long as the two basic ones just described are present.

181

Unit

The amenities in the unit itself cover a tremendous range and greatly add to or detract from its value. In my opinion, there are some basic features that should be present in all your investment condo units:

- Central air conditioning and heating.

- Laundry facilities: Even if they're just a combination washer/dryer unit sitting in a hallway alcove.

- Bathrooms: A unit with more than one bedroom should have at least two bathrooms; one should have a tub, the other, a shower stall.

- Kitchen facilities: An oven and range, a garbage disposal, dishwasher, ceramic tile or formica countertops, and adequate cupboard space.

- Good quality wall-to-wall carpeting in a neutral tone.

- Space: At least 700 square feet for one-bedroom and 900 square feet for two-bedroom units.

- Location: Away from stairways or elevators; an end unit is nearly always the best location.

Rental Income

As you research your vacancy factor, you will also determine the potential income of your proposed investment. Follow these steps:

1. Survey the neighborhood.

2. Posing as a potential renter, call on newspaper ads offering units for rent comparable to your potential purchase.

3. Determine whether your potential unit's income will cover the six major expense items—homeowner fees, taxes, insurance, interior maintenance, mortgage payments, and vacancy factor.

If the potential rental income will not cover those items, you will have a negative cash flow—more cash going out than coming in. To alleviate a negative cash flow, you have to reduce expenses or increase income. The only expense item you can directly influence is your mortgage payment. Your mortgage payment is determined by the price you pay for the unit and your down payment. After you've obtained the best adjustable-rate or fixed-rate financing available and have negotiated a rock bottom price for the unit, if the investment still doesn't pay for itself, find another unit to buy. Don't settle for a problem!

Multiphased Projects

Soon there will be another housing construction boom. Prices will edge up. Condos, co-ops, and single family housing tracts will spring up everywhere. To prepare you for that golden opportunity, I'm going to let you in on an investment strategy that could make you a lot of money. It's simple to get into—so simple, in fact, you'll wonder why "everybody" doesn't do it. Well, everybody doesn't do it because everybody doesn't know about it. Those who do know about it do it, and do it frequently. But it can be done only under the right market condition: A highly appreciating seller's market.

The strategy is applicable both to new single family housing tracts and new condo or co-op projects. I've made money from them all!

Here's how it works: When a development company begins a project of, say, 50 units and up, they complete the project in phases. In phase one, they may complete 25 percent of the project and sell it out. In phase two, 40 percent, and so forth, until the whole project is completely built and sold. The percentages I've given are not important. What's important is the fact that there are different *stages* of the project's completion.

For each phase after the first one, the developer will normally increase the price per unit. What you want to do is buy in phase one, when prices are at their lowest. Typically, phase two will be priced up to 20 percent higher, and phase three, higher again. If it's a new condo complex, you may have to buy from a floor plan. If it's a single family housing tract, you'll see a floor plan, select a lot, and choose an elevation. (*Elevation* refers to the exterior design of the house.) In either case, you're most likely going to be buying something before it's even built.

Before you engage in this plan, however, make certain you know comparable prices in the area. You should do a market survey the same as if you were preparing to purchase a resale house or condo. Don't jump headlong into something before you do all your homework. But, as soon as you've located the project you're interested in and feel secure that the development company's opening prices compare favorably with your comps, you can enter into a purchase contract. The development company will love you for that! As many presales as the company can get will put them in good stead with their lender. The lender will be gratified to know that the development company is constructing an attractive, salable product.

Usually, you will be required to put up about 3 percent of the unit's cost as an earnest money deposit. That money should be placed into an escrow account. Never—but *never*—give the earnest money deposit to the development company. About six to eight months later, during which time you will have expended no additional funds, your unit will be nearing completion. About the same time, the builder will be getting out publicity and making arrangements to sell the phase two homes, which the builder is about to start. Phase two will normally cost about 20 percent more than phase one in an appreciating market. As soon as you know the builder's price of phase two, you'll put your unit up for sale at a price a little less than the phase two properties but much greater than your purchase contract. When you find a buyer, you simply enter into a sale agreement with that buyer with the added contingency "subject to seller acquiring title." Your buyer will put his or her deposit money into the same escrow company that you engaged with the development company. You will then instruct your escrow officer to close your purchase escrow concurrently with your sale escrow. Then, you pocket the difference in cash! How's that for making money?

Here's the process for a three-bedroom, two-bath condo:

1. Compile comps to confirm the fairness of the developer's $145,000 price for the condo.

2. Enter into a contract with the developer to purchase.

3. Place 3 percent ($4,350) deposit money in escrow.

4. As soon as the developer announces phase two prices, you offer your unit for sale for a little less. Phase two prices may be as much as 20 percent higher or, in our example, $174,000.

5. You price your unit at $168,000.

6. You find a buyer and enter into a sale contract for $168,000 with the contingency "subject to seller acquiring title."

7. You go to escrow and instruct your escrow officer to close your purchase and sale escrow concurrently.

8. At the close of escrow, you pocket the difference of your $145,000 purchase price and your $168,000 sale price: $23,000, less costs of escrow.

9. What's your profit? About 400 percent on your $4,350 investment!

Can you make money by buying into phase two? Sure, but I think it's a bit more risky. In my experience, the greatest price increase occurred between phases one and two.

Tax Implications of Condo and Co-op Investments

The 1986 Tax Reform Act imposed some limitations on the formerly benefit-laden tax ride that most real estate investors enjoyed. In the "good old days," real estate losses in excess of real estate income could be summarily deducted from ordinary income. It was a terrific situation, because even though you had an investment that was breaking even on a cash basis, you could still enjoy the yearly paper deduction of depreciation from your ordinary income. That simple calculation substantially reduced taxes and contributed greatly in making real estate a very attractive form of investment.

The Tax Reform Act of 1986

While not totally obliterated, that benefit is now a bit more difficult to enjoy. The fundamental change the 1986 Tax Reform Act imposed on investment real estate was to classify the residential rental business as a "passive" activity. That designation meant that any loss beyond the income the property produced couldn't be deducted from ordinary income. The act says you have to defer that loss to an ensuing year when you may show a cash profit. Or you can accumulate several years' losses and deduct them from your profit when you finally sell the property.

The elimination of the deduction from ordinary income, if left alone, could have dealt a serious blow to the real estate investment business. However, the act amended itself somewhat by adding the following modifications. You can change the classification of your real estate business from "passive" to "active." With an "active" classification, you can restore some of the old familiar tax benefits for yourself.

How does one go about doing that? Quite simply. To have an "active" classification, you must own more than 10 percent of the property and be personally involved in its operation. Personal involvement means you must "do" something—collect rents, supervise refurbishing, select tenants, write advertisements, and other tasks.

But, that's not all. Another modification involves the total amount of your adjusted gross income; your normal sources of income less allowable deductions. The act says that if your adjusted gross income is less than $100,000, you can deduct up to $25,000 of your rental operational losses. It also allows that if your adjusted gross income exceeds $100,000, then for every dollar you exceed $100,000, you can take a 50-cent deduction. When you reach $150,000, the $25,000-deduction limit is eliminated entirely.

Depreciation

Being newly initiated to real estate investing, you may not fully comprehend the use of the term *depreciation*. You might ask, for instance, "If property normally appreciates over the years, why are we talking about depreciation?" Well, the answer is that taking depreciation in reality is the act of recovering the cost of your investment over a period of time. Currently, the government allows you to do that at the rate of 3.6 percent per year for 27.5 years. If you sell anywhere within that time period, your buyer can begin the whole depreciation process over again, according to his or her new basis.

Ways to Accumulate Wealth from Condos and Co-ops

Buy entry-level distressed properties in well-maintained and centrally located buildings at 15 to 20 percent below your calculated future net sales price. After you refurbish them then, you will, in effect, have created your own "instant appreciation." Even if your unit operated at a breakeven point, the paper write-off of depreciation could possibly result in a reduction of your income tax responsibility. If you rent the property out for several years, appreciation and mortgage reduction will increase your equity in the unit. It's very possible that over a period of time, your rental income will exceed your monthly expenses, resulting in a net cash flow.

The tax-free realization of cash from refinancing can be accomplished when the unit's loan balance is reduced to around 60 percent of its market value. With a new loan of 75 to 80 percent of that value, you can pocket the net cash for additional investments.

The Glorious Small Apartment Building

Beginning in the 1960s, my wife Patty and I were in the apartment house business in the San Fernando Valley area of Los Angeles, an experience that spanned more than two decades. During that period we dealt with a whole kaleidoscope of experiences—some good, some not so good. To paraphrase Dickens, "They were the worst of times and they were the best of times." The "worst of times" taught us perseverance and patience; the "best of times" confirmed our faith in the power of positive thinking.

Besides enjoying some spectacular increases in the values of our properties during that era, we had some bitter pills to swallow as well. High vacancy factors, a tight money supply, exorbitant interest rates—they all threatened our prosperity at one time or another. But, we stood firm and prevailed.

You may ask, "Was it worth all that?" You bet it was. How else could we, two people starting together with nothing more than $2,600 and lots of guts, become millionaires while we were still young enough to enjoy it?

The opportunities in the ownership and operation of apartments are still robust. With the help of some of the sources of investment capital I revealed earlier, almost anyone can enter the business on a part-time basis. And, by using the methods explained in this chapter, success will be practically ensured. "Will there be some difficult periods?" Yes, count on them. "Will the temptation to quit arise?" Yes. No one's impervious to mental anguish. "Will seemingly unsurmountable impediments come along?" Yes. But, if you maintain a positive attitude, you'll make them disappear.

I call an apartment house *small* if it has between 6 and 15 units. In most urban communities, newer properties in that size range, well located, and free of deferred maintenance are the most hotly pursued investments. They are usually accessible to a great number of "trophy" buyers. Trophy buyers are people who invest in pride-of-ownership properties basically to feed their egos. There's nothing wrong with that. But, I'd rather *make* trophies than buy them. Trophies usually don't make the best investments because people bid their prices too high.

What you as a smart investor want to do is avoid getting into a bidding contest. Never increase your evaluation of a building merely because someone else is coming in with a higher offer.

I suggest that rather than going after those trophies, you create them by investing in properties in desperate need of repair and making them beautiful. As long as they are in a stable neighborhood, without structural deficiencies, and needing only a cosmetic facelift, you will make money—lots of it. Those are the kinds of properties my wife Patty and I bought—the "trophy" hunter's rejects.

Sources of Distressed Apartment Houses

Real Estate Owned by Banks and Savings and Loans

Not often, but occasionally, apartment houses show up as REOs. It doesn't happen often because most apartment house owners are sophisticated enough to sell their property before the death knell of foreclosure falls on them. However, in order to be aware of the few that may show up, subscribe to a professional legal newspaper that publishes trustee sales. Besides the address of the property and the lender, the notice will give the name and phone number of the trustee who will conduct the sale.

After the sale date has elapsed, assuming you did not personally attend the event to witness what happened, call the trustee and ask if the property was indeed purchased.

If no trustee sale was consummated, visit the property. If it outwardly appears to qualify as being distressed, contact the lender's office. Ask for the "real estate owned" department. When you reach a loan officer, explain that you are interested in the property and would like some information about it.

From the notice in the paper, you will be aware of its financial condition, but you must ask for other needed information; its rental income, monthly utility bills, gardening or pool fees, taxes, and insurance premiums. You'll also want to know whether there are any vacant units and, if so, the length of time they've been vacant.

With that information, you will be prepared to do a property analysis to determine whether the purchase will make you money. If it works out, make an offer. I'll illustrate the way I prepared apartment house analyses later in this chapter.

Auctions

The use of the auction to sell everything from antiques to real estate has grown in popularity by leaps and bounds. Although the results are not in the least guaranteed, it's possible to get good buys on apartment houses at auctions. A lot depends on the condition of the marketplace and the degree of urgency facing the seller. Don't assume that all owners putting their property up for auction are desperate for a sale. Many of them use the auction merely as another marketing alternative.

What single important detail will most impact the success or failure of your prospective auction purchase? The thoroughness of your research. Without an exhaustive investigation of the property up for auction, you'll not be able to recognize whether you're confronting a good deal.

Auctions are advertised far in advance of the dates on which they actually occur. As soon as you see an auction ad for a property that interests you, send for its advertised brochure. Then, take advantage of the interim time to do a thorough research job. The proper calculations and evaluation procedures are given later in this chapter. Use them. Know the top dollar you can pay to achieve a good deal and don't waiver from your decision—no matter how heated the bidding becomes. I've been there and I know: Many people pay above-market prices for auctioned properties. They get carried away with the bidding process and end up behind the eight ball!

Newspaper Ads

Many terrific, money-making properties are listed in the real estate classified ad section of the weekend editions of local newspapers. Opportunity words like "partnership dissolving," "illness forces sale," "divorce," "owner retiring," "owner relocating," could mean the sellers are anxious to deal. Contact the real estate agencies involved, then visit the properties to see whether they lie in a suitable location. If they do, and they appear ripe for renovation, you will have found your pearl in the oyster.

How to Evaluate an Apartment House

Exterior Deferred Maintenance

As a rule, owners won't readily admit to any deferred maintenance existing on their property. You have to observe for yourself. Start with the outward appearance of the property: Peeling paint, missing window screens, inadequate rubbish collection facilities, unsafe staircases, asphalt driveways wrinkled with cracks, a dead or dying landscape, garages laden with trash—you get the idea? Those and many other deficiencies mark a property suffering from deferred maintenance. As long as they're all surface or "cosmetic" problems, a little clean-up money along with some creativity can turn the place into one fit for the trophy hunters.

Physical Facilities

Most small apartment buildings have at least one or two washer and drier machines located in a laundry room. The condition of the laundry room may reflect the overall condition of the building.

If the machines are leased, the lessor usually has the responsibility to maintain the room. If not, the appearance of the room is left to the owner. On an inspection tour, a messy, lint-laden laundry room may discourage fussy prospective tenants from desiring to reside in the building.

The laundry room usually houses the building's water heater. Check the date that it was installed. With a life expectancy of about 20 years, you may be buying the property just in time to install a new one.

If there's a pool on the property, pay a pool maintenance professional a fee to evaluate its condition. If you're going to need a new motor, filter, or heater, you need to know that in order to bargain your purchase price.

House Vacancies

As you enter the property, note the mailboxes. You can get a fairly good idea about the number of vacancies in the building by noting how many mailboxes are without names. Also note the gas meters located toward the front of the building. Vacant apartments will have their gas meters tagged by the utility company.

Neighborhood Vacancies

Survey the neighborhood for vacancies. You want to know not only the number out there, their sizes, and how many built-in amenities they have but their rental rates as well. Look at buildings that will compare to your proposed purchase after it's refurbished.

Vacancy information will influence your price negotiations. The more the vacancy factor surpasses 5 percent, the lower you'll want to bid.

Unit Inspection

Usually, you cannot ask to inspect the interior of individual units in a building unless you make an offer to buy. Therefore, always make your offer subject to your approval of each unit after inspection. And you must in fact inspect *each* unit. Never accept the seller's statement: "This unit is the same as the one downstairs, so you don't have to bother looking at that one." The unit downstairs could be a total disaster. It's always best to insist on seeing each one. You can prepare a checklist of things to look for much the same as the one used to inspect a single family home.

Management

In a smaller apartment house, you usually will not find a resident or off-site manager. The building's income just wouldn't support that expense. Generally, a building must have more than 10 units before it can begin to afford outside or on-site management. Therefore, in a smaller building, you can't blame a manager for the distressed state of the property. Most likely, the fault will lie with the owner. Lack of interest, lack of money, poor health, partnership conflicts—any number of reasons could account for a building's state of deterioration. The worse part is that deterioration attracts bad tenants and drives good ones away, thereby perpetrating the property's decrepit appearance.

Parking

Garage space and extra parking are an integral part of a successful apartment house. The first questions prospective tenants ask me are, "How many garage spaces go with the unit?" "Is there any extra parking?" Most apartment houses have one garage or carport per unit. Usually, extra parking can be accommodated only on the street. Therefore, try to select a building located on a street that does not have "no parking" signs posted.

Location

The location of an apartment house is crucial to its success. Find one in a residential area close to public transportation and within easy freeway access. I particularly like buildings located within walking distance of mini shopping malls. That way, trips to the cleaners, hair salon, and pharmacy will be reachable on foot.

I don't advocate that anyone buy an apartment house that is half of a twin complex. Southern California contains many projects of that configuration. For instance, if you see a trashed out eight-unit building sharing a common courtyard with its twin, it's not a good idea to buy that property. No matter how well you renovate your side of the courtyard, your possibly messy neighbor will seriously detract from your efforts. Remember, if you can't control your total environment, don't buy. The same warning applies to purchasing a distressed property surrounded by other distressed properties. Don't do it.

Instead, purchase the "ugly duckling" surrounded by trophies.

Rental Income

Generally, the price of an apartment house is based on its current income—emphasis on current! Never buy a building at a price based on its future or "projected" income. You'll be surprised at the number of brokers who list a property with serious deferred maintenance problems, then ask a buyer to purchase that property at a price based on the rental income the building will generate after all the improvements are completed.

Always make your offer to purchase with the contingency "subject to verification of the current rents and approval of all rental agreements and leases." Even after reading the rental agreements and leases, verify everything with the tenants—just to be sure no unwritten "understandings" exist.

"Why is knowing each rental rate so important?" Well, the owner wants to sell at the highest price possible. That owner knows that the sale price is based on the building's income. Even if he or she misstates the building's yearly income by only a few hundred dollars, it can mean several thousand dollars added to the sale price, distorting its true value. Later, in this chapter, when you learn how to price a building, you'll understand how that can happen.

Verification of monthly rent and other terms of tenancy can be accomplished by having each tenant sign an information statement—sometimes referred to as an "offset" statement. Each unit's tenant can do that as you inspect the premises. The "offset" statement should include the following information:

- Unit number and garage or parking area number

- Names of tenants within the unit

- Number of children and adults occupying the unit

- Pets

- Type of tenancy: Lease or month to month

- Amount of money on deposit with owner:
  (a) last month's rent
  (b) security deposit

- Monthly rental rate

- Included in rent:
  (a) utilities: water, gas, and electric
  (b) stove and refrigerator
  (c) other

- Rental due date

- Tenant's signature affirming accuracy of the information

- The current date

Furnishings

When you purchase an apartment house, the only furnishings I believe you should consider are stoves and refrigerators. Dinette sets, living room and bedroom furnishings have almost no real value, even though their use in the apartments may bring in a larger monthly rental rate. The higher vacancy factor associated with furnished units more than eats up the increased rental income.

Furnished units make it too easy for people to move, creating an almost constant tenant turnover. In Southern California, furnished apartment houses operate just one step above motels! The constant recurring costs of cleaning, painting, repairing, and furniture replacement are too high and consume too much time to make furnished units worthwhile.

If you find a good distressed building whose units happen to be furnished, base your purchase price on the rental value of the apartments *without* furniture.

How to Calculate the Price of an Apartment House

After you've thoroughly checked out your prospective distressed building, you arrive at the point of trying to determine its value. In the good old days, when life was easier, it was a common practice among apartment investors to simply base the value of a building at six to eight times its yearly gross income. It wasn't a foolproof method, but it gave a ballpark number from which one could begin negotiations. In the San Fernando Valley of Los Angeles, it was a fairly common practice to pay six times the gross or less if the building were older, neglected, in a marginal low-rental-demand area, and to pay eight times the gross if it were newer, in good condition, and in a better, high-rental-demand area. Even if, by using that rather feeble rule-of-thumb method, the investor ended up paying too much for the building, the income tax benefits available at that time eased somewhat the pain of the over-generous purchase price.

Those days, dear reader, are gone. The salutary real estate tax benefits, although not entirely eliminated, have been seriously curtailed. Under the Tax Reform Act of 1986, you can no longer deduct unlimited apartment house operational losses from your adjusted gross income.

Because of the enactment of the 1986 Tax Reform Act, determining the *proper* purchase price of an apartment house has become crucial. The old "times gross" rule of thumb is obsolete and should never be used as a legitimate method to evaluate the value of an apartment house in today's environment. Let's proceed now to learn a couple of evaluation techniques that do give a good indication of the value of a building.

The Capitalization Rate System

Several numerical factors differ from building to building. Operating expenses, income, mortgage interest rates, and the vacancy factor—all play an integral part in the evaluation of a building. Even if you had two identically constructed buildings standing side by side, there could be a significant difference in their individual fiscal outlines. Any system of evaluation that doesn't take those individual differences into account lacks reliability and authenticity.

The capitalization rate system, which takes into account a building's expenses, income, and vacancy factor, has been used for a long time to measure the value of a building. In order to illustrate how it works, I'll describe a sample property to which it can be applied: "Regal House."

This property consists of 10 units, all with two bedrooms and two baths. They each rent for $800 per month. There are no current vacancies, although they lie in an area that usually experiences a yearly vacancy factor of 4.5 percent. The building is about 20 years old and in dire need of cosmetic repairs.

Regal House Income

$	8,000	Ten units at $800 per month
−	360	Vacancy factor of 4.5%
+	75	Monthly laundry income
$	7,715	Monthly effective gross income
×	12	Months of rent and laundry income per year
$	92,580	Yearly effective gross income

Expenses

$	37,080	Taxes, insurance utilities, trash pick-up, gardener, and maintenance (approximately 40% of yearly effective gross income)
$	55,500	Yearly net income

The "net income" of our sample building is $55,500. It's what's left over *before* deducting the mortgage payments and is the first key number we need in order to use the capitalization rate system.

The second key number, called the "cap rate," is an arbitrary percentage. In the recent past, I usually pegged it at 10 percent—two points above the 8 percent money market rate available at the time.

However, at this writing, the money market rate is down to 4 percent. To have a cap rate of only two points higher will result in your paying too much for a building.

The lower the cap rate, the higher the indicated value. The higher the cap rate, the lower the indicated value.

Basically, you want as high a cap rate as practical. Consult with real estate appraisers. Ask what they're doing in the locations you're interested in. In all likelihood, the lender you'll use will base the size of loan on what the local appraisers say and do anyway. Therefore, it may be to your advantage to use their cap rate percentage to calculate the value of a building. You can contact appraisers under the "real estate appraisers" heading in your Yellow Pages. Try to locate an apartment house specialist.

Cap rates differ from one area of the country to another. They may even differ for two adjacent cities, depending on the customs of each locale. Especially in areas of limited apartment house sale activity, cap rates may be extracted after the fact, from recently sold buildings.

The rationale for the cap rate is as follows: If you had $10,000 in an account at a bank or S&L and you agreed to the institution's terms, your $10,000 could possibly earn anywhere from 5 to 8 percent interest yearly. Without compounding interest, the yield would amount to between $500 and $800.

Let's look at that from another angle. Suppose someone offered you $800 interest on an undisclosed sum of investment capital. Say you wanted that $800 to represent 8 percent interest on your investment. How much capital would you have to invest for that return? To get that answer, you'd divide $800 by the 8 percent rate of return. Your quotient—or answer—would be $10,000:

$$\$800 \div 0.08 = \$10,000$$

Now, if you wanted that $800 to represent a 10 percent return on your investment, you would have to invest only $8,000:

$$\$800 \div 0.10 = \$8,000$$

When the time comes to invest in an apartment house, you may reason, "Well, if a practically no-risk bank account could possibly earn 8 percent, I want at least 10 percent on risk capital." Let's apply that reasoning to the prospective purchase of our sample apartment house. The building's net income represents your investment capital.

Take the net income of $55,500 and divide it by the capitalization rate of 10 percent. The answer is

$$\$55,500 \div 0.10 = \$555,000$$

So, $555,000 is the "cap rate" value of our sample building.

Caution: The cap rate system is usually not applicable to buildings of fewer than 5 units. The cost per unit of such properties is way out of proportion to the income that they can generate. For instance, in Southern California, a 10-unit building may cost about $500,000, or $50,000 per unit. Yet, if you were to price a duplex with apartments of similar size and amenities, you'd have to pay $80,000 and up per unit. Both apartments in both buildings would produce approximately the same rental income.

I call buildings of fewer than five units "renter-assisted" properties. They function primarily as owner-occupied but enjoy the advantage of having rent-paying tenants help cover the costs of the mortgage and expenses.

The way to price such buildings is either by employing a professional appraiser or by doing a market survey to find out what similar properties have sold for recently.

Now, let's learn another system of evaluation—one that I used throughout my investment career. I call it the "breakeven system."

The Breakeven System

Whereas the "cap rate" system gave a property value that took into account the building's expenses, income, and vacancy factor, the breakeven system goes one step further. It accounts for the building's future encumbrance after purchase.

Under the assumption that you will apply for a new loan when you make your purchase, the breakeven system tells you how much of a new loan the building's current income can pay for after meeting all the other expenses and the vacancy factor. The new loan, plus the negotiable down payment, will indicate the highest price you could offer for the building and yet break even.

According to the listed information of our sample apartment house, the expenses are $3,090 per month ($37,080 ÷ 12). That number represents about 40 percent of the building's gross income. That's a pretty fair percentage. I would look askance at the listing of an older, neglected building that gave an expense percentage that was less than 40 percent of income.

Let's proceed. If you deduct $3,090 of expenses from the monthly effective gross income of $7,715, your answer is $4,625. That's the total amount of monthly income you could use for a monthly loan payment and still break even. The question now is, What principal loan amount has payments of $4,625 per month?

To answer that question, you need a mortgage rate factor booklet. They are available in stationery stores, your library or are free from some title companies. It's a very handy reference tool to have, because the booklet gives you the monthly cost per $1,000 for a loan at various lengths of time and at various interest rates.

For instance, a sum of money loaned for 30 years at a yearly interest rate of 10.25 percent costs $8.97 per thousand per month. Therefore, a $100,000 loan for 30 years at 10.25 percent would cost $897 (100 × $8.97) per month.

Let's put it another way: If you had a building that could afford $897 per month for a loan payment, what is the largest loan amount available at 10.5 percent interest for 30 years? Your answer would be derived by dividing $897 by $8.97 or 100. One hundred times a thousand dollars is $100,000.

To apply that factor to our sample property, you would divide $4,625 by $8.97 for an answer of 515.607. If you multiply 515.607 times 1,000, for $515,607, that figure would be the highest loan the building could afford to pay for out of its current monthly income.

Obviously, if you selected a lower interest rate, the factor would be lower and the loan amount larger. That's why I believe this method helps an investor. It takes into account the "cost" of money. The loan, which usually represents a significant portion of the price of a building, influences the value of a building. The higher the cost of financing, the lower the value of the building.

Now, after you've determined the breakeven loan figure, you're ready for the next step in the evaluation process. What you know so far is that in order to operate without a negative cash flow, you should not encumber the building for more than $515,607.

However, just because that is the highest loan the building can afford, it isn't necessarily the loan amount you *want*. You want to negotiate a price that will give you a smaller loan with a smaller monthly payment so that you can build a cash reserve at the end of each month.

We determined the cap rate evaluation to be $555,000, while the breakeven system, gave us a maximum loan of $515,607. The

$555,000 represents the cap rate price for the entire property—loan and down payment combined. The $515,607 represents only part of the cost of the property—the loan. The other part—the down payment—is subject to negotiation.

If you figure that at best the $515,607 loan represents a 90 percent loan to value ratio, with a 10 percent down payment, your purchase price would be about $572,897 ($515,607 ÷ 0.9 = $572,897).

Between a low price of $555,000 and a high one of $572,897 is where you should attempt to strike a deal.

With a 10 percent down payment, if you exceed the price of $572,897, you'll be operating with a negative cash flow; if you buy for less, you could end up with a monthly cash reserve.

By increasing your down payment, thereby lowering your loan amount, you could also end up with a monthly cash flow.

How to Increase the Value of an Apartment House

Everything considered, there is really only one way to increase the value of an apartment house: raise the rental income. However, some cities have rent-control ordinances of various degrees of severity that restrict your ability to do that. In those cities, you simply cannot arbitrarily decide to raise everyone's rent.

In variance with what I said earlier about keeping your investment properties close to where you live, if your city has a rent-control ordinance that does not include "vacancy decontrol," invest elsewhere. Vacancy decontrol means that after a tenant voluntarily moves out of a unit, you, the owner, have the right to rerent the apartment at the highest market rate available. A few cities across America have rent-control ordinances that do not permit that.

Even if you live in a city that has no rent control, I advise you not to buy a building and then, at the close of escrow, issue all the tenants a 30-day rent increase notice. That act could drive away some good-paying tenants and put you in bad stead with the rest.

If you buy the kind of property I've been advocating, you're going to be buying a building in a rather wretched state of disrepair. To raise your tenants' rents without addressing the building's problems first is just bad business.

Rehab the Exterior

Here's a better way to proceed. As soon as the building is yours, you should begin the exterior renovations. For instance, if the wood trim needs painting, do it. You'd be surprised how that simple correction alone can spruce up the appearance of a building.

If you have cracked exterior staircases, tackle that job next. In Southern California, we have many apartment houses with exterior staircases made of diata—a white, cement-like substance that looks great new but tends to crack over time, producing a very unpleasant visual defect. However, the cracks can be filled by a skilled craftsperson and a decent paint job restores them to their original luster.

Clearing the garages of all trash should be included among the first rehab items. I usually gave all my tenants a week's warning that anything not stored in the garage cabinets will be taken away by the trash pickup. Some tenants treat the garage area as their personal junkyard. Unless you force them to secure their belongings, the place will never look neat and clean.

About the same time you do the garage area, you should tackle the asphalt driveway. If there are many hair-line cracks present, for a rather minimum cost, a good paving company can apply a thin oil coating that will fill them in, thus restoring a very decent appearance. If there are serious cracks, however, you'll have to completely resurface the area at a considerably higher price.

Landscaping was my specialty. I always strove to give a parklike appearance to the grounds of all my buildings. Most of the time, I was able to accomplish a lot of that by removing dead or dying shrubs and trees. Then, I would extend the lawn into those areas. I tried to create as much lawn surface as possible, because I think expansive lawns give a building a very "classy" look.

Don't spend a lot of money on annuals—shrubs and flowers that have only one seasonal lifespan. Use the more durable perennials. Overall, they cost less because they don't have to be replaced yearly and they're easier to maintain by the average gardener. Landscaping is the one physical aspect of a property that attracts the most desirable tenants. Give it a lot of attention and reap the rewards.

Renovate the Interior

Now, let's talk about interior renovations. When should you do them? Only as the units become vacant through natural tenant turnover. What should you do? As much as needed to create the appearance of a brand new unit and beat out your competition.

Vacancies: Positive, Not Negative, Events

Positive thinking says vacancies provide more of a golden opportunity than a fiscal hardship. Vacancies give you the opportunity to renovate; renovation increases the building's income; increased income raises a building's value; higher value increases your equity.

During the gap between a former tenant leaving and a new tenant occupying the unit—in other words, the normal tenant turnover—is the best time to refurbish a unit. It should be your intention to ultimately refurbish each unit to gain maximum income. Avoid rendering hardships to existing tenants by giving them rent increases before you improve their apartments.

Tenants living in substandard units cannot afford a rent raise. If they could afford a higher rent, they wouldn't be living there! Therefore, I do not advocate doing a complete renovation on an occupied unit. Even if the tenants agreed to a higher rent after making the improvements, their tenancy won't last long. After a couple of months they'll leave, and you'll have the work to do all over again.

If your apartments are in an area of very slow tenant turnover, then and only then should you resort to issuing occupants 30-day notices to vacate.

Renovations: How Much Is Enough?

The amount and quality of interior renovations you do should reflect the amount of rent you expect to receive. Aim for top dollar. Visit vacant apartments in your immediate area. Take notes of what others have done—then make yours a little better. Get inexpensive ideas from home improvement magazines. Sometimes one little feature will be the detail that sets your unit apart from those of your competition.

One rather inexpensive feature I started adding was carpeting in bathrooms. While everyone else was putting in cheap linoleum, my carpeted bathrooms looked very luxurious. The "look" far exceeded the cost.

Another idea I had was to wallpaper one wall of the dining area. It created a little special effect that caught the tenant's eye but was inexpensive to do. How about new door knobs, updated plumbing fixtures, a couple of contemporary light fixtures, or miniblinds instead of draperies? Do something special to make the unit appear to be brand new. Experiment for yourself and have fun doing it.

Now that you understand the importance of refurbishing the exterior and interior of an apartment house to gain the highest possible income, let's see how that pays off for you—how you gain from it.

Apartment House Ownership: The Fast Track to Millions

When I took you through the cap rate and breakeven methods of determining the value of an apartment house, gross income played a vital role. By now, I'm sure you understand that the greater the gross income, the more valuable the building. What you may not realize, however, is the extent to which every dollar of monthly rental increase affects value. Let's look at our sample building again:

$	8,000	10 units at $800 per month
–	360	Vacancy factor of 4.5%
+	75	Monthly laundry income
$	7,715	Total monthly effective gross income
×	12	Months of income per year
$	92,580	Yearly effective gross income

With a yearly effective gross income of $92,580, using the cap rate and breakeven systems of evaluation, I showed you that the building's value ranged between a low of $555,000 and a high of $572,897.

Now after making all the exterior and interior improvements, the monthly rental rate could rise from $800 to $880 per unit. That 10 percent increase should be relatively easy to achieve in all units in less than 30 months. Let's see how that increase translates into a building's value.

$	8,800	10 units' rent at $880 per month
–	396	Vacancy factor of 4.5%
+	75	Monthly laundry income
$	8,479	Total monthly effective gross income
×	12	Months of income per year
$	101,748	Yearly effective gross income

Cap Rate Value:

$	101,748	Yearly effective gross income
–	37,080	Annual expenses
$	64,668	Yearly net income
$	646,680	Cap rate value (yearly net income ÷ 0.10)

Breakeven Value:

$	8,479	Monthly effective gross income
–	3,090	Monthly expenses
$	5,389	Net monthly income available for debt service
$	600,780	Breakeven loan value (net monthly income ÷ factor for a 10.25% loan for 30 years, or $5,389 ÷ 8.97 = $600,780)

The $600,780 represents the highest loan amount the building can afford with its new income stream. That number could also represent 90 percent of the value of the building with 10 percent down.

Therefore:

$600,780 ÷ 0.9 = $667,533, the breakeven value.

From a purchase value range of $555,000 to $572,897 to a new range of $646,680 to $667,533 is a formidable difference!

Going for the Gold: Trading Up to a Larger Building

In order to demonstrate how this sample property performed financially, let's go back to the beginning. We'll assume our purchase price for Regal House was $565,000, about halfway between the cap rate and breakeven values. Let's also assume we put 10 percent down, $56,500, and took out a new mortgage for $508,500 ($565,000 – $56,500) at 10.25 percent for 30 years.

Two and a half years later, as a result of rehabilitation efforts, the income has grown steadily from $8,000 to $8,800 per month. Using the same evaluation techniques as before, the building now has a value ranging between $646,680 and $667,533, as shown by the prior calculations. If we sold at halfway between those two figures, our sale price would be about $657,000, and our equity would be about $148,500 ($657,000 – $508,500).

The original down payment at the time of purchase was $56,500. That represented our total equity. Now, 30 months later, that equity has nearly tripled in value. Of course, in order to increase the income we had to pay for improvements. If, liberally speaking, it took $2,500 per unit for interior repairs and another $5,000 for the exterior renovation, the total expenditure for the property was as follows:

$	25,000	10 units at $2,500 each
+	5,000	Exterior rehab
$	30,000	Total rehab costs
+	56,500	Original down payment
$	86,500	Total invested

The current equity of $148,500 less the invested capital of $86,500 equals $62,000—nearly a 72 percent return over a 2.5-year period.

For the highly motivated investor seeking the status of "millionaire," this deal could be the first leg of the trip to financial stardom. Using the sophisticated techniques of the tax-deferred exchange, the investor is now ready to enter into a trade agreement for a larger building. He or she could use the formidable equity of $148,500 as the 10 percent down payment (less expenses of sale) for the purchase of a $1,250,000 distressed property.

Making the same kinds of improvements on the trade-up building as were done on the first building, in another 30 months the investor could double the equity. Estimating that he or she started with about $125,000, 10 percent down, on the trade-up building, in 2.5 years or less the investor would have a whopping $250,000 equity.

In awe of his or her own success, the investor will surely decide to go for the gold—"millionaire" status. By taking the $250,000 equity and repeating the process about two more times, the equity will expand to more than $1 million.

"Is this really possible?" you ask. Yes, it's really possible. If you invest in distressed buildings, use maximum but safe leverage, and apply your rehabilitation money prudently, this example can be replicated over and over again.

The actual timetable to achieve millionaire status may not conform exactly to this illustration. The real estate market fluctuates for and against the investor's timetable. For instance, there could be a period where it would not be possible to trade up because financing terms were unmanageable, or, on the plus side, our investor may be able to accomplish rent increases over a shorter period of time. Alternatively, the investor could get more than a 10 percent increase in the rents after rehabilitation. There are any number of things that could happen to alter the illustrated timetable. But, if our investor remembers the three Ps—patience, persistence, and positive thinking—millionaire status will be obtainable in a very reasonable length of time.

The Business of Real Estate Recordkeeping

We live in a world where keeping accurate records is absolutely essential for doing business. It's a task most people would prefer to avoid. But face it, as long as "Big Brother" is constantly looking over our shoulders, the chore of recordkeeping will not go away. What records to keep, how to keep them, and for how long is the subject of this chapter.

I'm going to begin by discussing the Internal Revenue Service (IRS). That's the agency that mandates so much of our recordkeeping. That's the agency to which you have to respond if, in the event of an audit, you cannot justify a challenged deduction. Here goes.

What the IRS Requires Us to Keep—
And for How Long

Recently, here in Southern California, the media was ablaze with a story about Willie Nelson. It seems that the IRS had targeted him for more than $16 million Willie owed in back taxes. It was the unfortunate consequence of some questionable tax shelter deductions he took over a decade ago. The headline stories led you to believe that Willie's problem had just recently surfaced, when in fact his case had been before the courts long before the media caught wind of it.

The truth is this: There is a set time period within which the IRS must bring charges against the taxpayer. Unless the taxpayer (or nontaxpayer!) is involved in a provable fraud, the IRS simply cannot keep a person on edge forever. There are three time frames within which charges must be levied, described here.

Situations Under the Three-Year Limit

After examining your return, if the IRS questions your deductions, they have three years from the date of filing or the date due, whichever is later, in which they can challenge you. However, of the 112 million returns filed in 1991, the IRS examined only 1,124,000— about 1 percent. I don't know what percentage of those examined ended up owing the government money, but if you are among those challenged, your possession of careful records could save you a lot of heartache and possibly a lot of money as well.

Situations Under the Six-Year Limit

The time period for IRS investigations is extended to six years if the service suspects that the income you reported is short by 25 percent or more of what you actually took in. However, if the IRS brings charges against you within the six-year time period, the agents can question not only your income but everything else as well.

Today, unreported income is not the moral quandary it once was. Through the use of the ubiquitous 1099 form, heretofore hidden sources of extra income such as real estate sales, interest, and dividends are now all routinely reported to the IRS by the agencies involved.

Situations with No Limits for Investigations

If you're suspected of deceiving the government—in other words, if the IRS believes you committed fraud—the rules change. The investigation of fraud is timeless. Fraud involves, for instance, the failure to file a return for a certain year or the act of claiming a dependent who doesn't exist. Fraud is a major issue; the IRS can add a civil penalty of 75 percent of whatever you owe plus interest from the date you incurred the liability.

To prosecute a taxpayer for fraud, the IRS must prove to the courts that from the onset, the taxpayer's intent was to maliciously deceive the government. If the taxpayer is found guilty of such a charge, the IRS could pursue criminal investigations that could result in incarceration.

Maintaining careful and complete records for each property you purchase should become second nature to you. You cannot evade or shirk the responsibility of being able to prove to the IRS every expenditure you claim as a deduction. There are two major classes of cash outlays you'll have to account for, which are covered next.

Capital Expenditures and Expenses of Operation

Capital Expenditures

A *capital expenditure* is a cash outlay that pays for permanent property improvements—something that increases the property's basis. I'll explain what "basis" is in a moment. A capital expenditure is not deductible on your tax return as a normal yearly cost of operation.

For instance, if you buy a distressed property and put on a new roof, the new roof will be added to the property's original cost. It will lower your reportable gain (profit) when you ultimately sell but will not qualify as a deductible expense item on your income tax forms in the year it was installed. The following is a list of other capital improvements you may have to make on the distressed properties I advocated you buy:

- New kitchen appliances
- New landscaping
- New heating and air conditioning units
- New block walls or other permanent fencing
- New pool equipment

Capital expenditures are expensive. If the distressed property you're contemplating buying needs too many of the items on this list, the costs may exceed the "5 percent of future sale price" improvement benchmark that I advocate. If they do, I suggest you find another property or lower your discount purchase price offer accordingly.

Now, let me explain what basis is. *Basis* is the term used to define the total cost of a property—the price you pay for it and the costs of its capital improvements rendered during your term of ownership. Your basis also includes the expenses of the purchase—recording fees, transfer taxes, title insurance, legal fees, and escrow charges. Later on, when you go to sell your property, the expenses of sale—real estate commission, escrow charges, and so on, will also be added to your basis. All those additions will serve to reduce your net reportable gain to the IRS.

Of course, you'll report a "gain" only on investment properties. For the sale of your personal residence, you'll most likely use the *rollover advantage*. That means, within certain guidelines, if you purchase another personal residence of equal or greater value than the one you sold, you will not have a reportable gain. The gain on your old house will be "rolled over" to the new one. Consult your CPA for more details.

---

*Maintain careful records of all
purchases, capital improvements,
rental income, operational expenses,
sale prices, and expenses of sale of
personal and investment properties.
Keep those records for six years
beyond the sale date of each property.*

The calculation of basis is important in another area—depreciation. In order to calculate the allowable depreciation deduction of your rental property, your CPA must know its basis.

Depreciation, which is the theoretical decline in value of a property mainly through age and usage, is in reality, something else. It's the government's way of allowing you, the investor, to recapture the cost of that property via a yearly deduction from its rental income. Currently, that deduction is about 3.6 percent of the cost of the property per year for 27.5 years.

In determining the basis of an investment property for depreciation purposes, you must deduct the value of its lot. Why? Only structures depreciate; land does not. As an example, let's say you bought a rental house for $150,000 and the lot on which it sits is valued at $35,000. The depreciable basis of the property is $115,000 ($150,000 − $35,000). The yearly allowable depreciation deduction of that property will be $4,182 ($115,000 ÷ 27.5).

Expenses

An *expense* is any other business-related cash outlay that's not a capital expenditure. The following are common expense items you're likely to have in the operation of your distressed property business:

- Interest on the loans
- Utilities

- Gardening and pool maintenance

- Emergency plumbing and electrical repairs

- Homeowner fees

- Insurance premiums

- Credit reports on prospective tenants

- Painting

- Carpet and drapery cleaning

- Depreciation

- Yearly allotment of loan points

Loan points, the cost of money, are treated as follows: For investment property, they are amortized over the life of the loan. For instance, if you get a $100,000 25-year loan on a distressed house and the lender charges you two points or $2,000, you will be allowed an annual deduction of $80 ($2,000 ÷ 25) for each year you own the property. See your CPA for all the current guidelines.

For the purchase of a personal residence, all the points charged are fully deductible in the year of purchase. However, if you refinance a personal residence, the points are amortized over the life of the loan just as they are for an investment property.

As you get started in this business, you'll be surprised at how quickly you'll accumulate "paper." Bills, loan payment receipts, insurance receipts—they're all important, and you have to keep track of them. Over the years, I've developed a recordkeeping technique that you may find useful. It's quite simple and involves maintaining looseleaf ledgers, folders, and envelopes. Those of you who are computer experts will, I'm sure, want to use your electronic equipment and some property management software to assist you in recordkeeping.

Let me explain the looseleaf ledgers first. I recommend a separate one for each property you own—your personal residence included. Title each one with the street name of the property. For example,

Cover: Rental: 4770 Cynthia Ave

Page 1:
  Description: 4 bedrooms 1½ baths
  Date of Purchase: Jan. 6, 1987
  Price: $115,000
  Complete address: 4770 Cynthia Ave,
                       Echo Valley, CA 91100
  Insurance:
    Agent: Jacobs and Son
    Phone: 818 213-4644
    Insurance Co.:   Metropolitan
    Policy Number: 07032
    Premium: $234

Page 2:   Cost of Purchase
Date: Escrow Co.:   Escrow Officer: Realtors:

Purchase price:
Realtor's commissions:
Attorney fees:
Escrow fees:
Title report:
Appraisal fee:
Transfer taxes:
Total of above: _____ (Basis After Purchase)

Page 3: Expenses of Rehab After Purchase
Date   Item   Contractor   Cost
Date   Item   Contractor   Cost
Date   Item   Contractor   Cost

Page 4: Capital Expenditures from Purchase Date to Sale Date
Basis after purchase: $_____
Date of expenditure   Item   Contractor   Cost
Total costs of capital expenditures to year's end _____
New basis at year's end   _____
(Calculate this basis yearly until the date of sale)

Page 5:   Maintenance Personnel
Gardener:
  Name
  Address
  Phone
  Monthly fee
  Duties
Pool attendant:
  Name
  Address
  Phone
  Monthly fee
  Duties

Page 6:   Rental Information
Tenant's name
Number of occupants
Date tenancy began
Lease or month-to-month rental agreement
Monthly rent
Rent includes
Last month's rent
Employer's name and address
Employer's phone number
Emergency phone number
Home phone number

Page 7:   Rental Income 199_

Date due	Date paid	Amount	How paid

Page 8:   Rental Expenses 199_

Date	Item	Payee	Amount*

*For each year, for each property keep a separate envelope containing all paid bills.

Page 9:
Sale Contacts
Listing date and Realtor
Sale date and Realtor
Time on market
List price
Sale price
Escrow company
Escrow officer

Improvements Made to Prepare the Property for Sale
Decorating
Draperies
Carpeting
Cleaning
Appliances
Landscaping

Escrow or Settlement Charges
Title insurance
Escrow fees
Legal fees
Transfer fees
Realtor's commission

Your CPA will need all this information in order to compute your net gain from the sale.

Besides a looseleaf ledger to record all the daily activities, keep three folders for each property. One will be your *Purchase* folder, which will contain your settlement papers from escrow, your note, and your trust deed. Later, if you refinance the property, keep all those papers in this folder also. Another one will be your *Sale* folder. It will contain all the settlement documents involved with the sale of the property. The third folder is the *Lease* folder, which safeguards leases or month-to-month rental agreements with your tenants.

This may seem like a lot to handle, but once you get into the system, it's easy. Make the process of writing entries in your ledgers a part of your daily routine. That way, maintaining the property's accounts will never become the arduous task they could be.

To be truly successful in this business, you have to pour yourself into it, even if you do it only part-time. For whatever time you devote to it, don't hold back—give it all you've got. Aren't you impressed at the single-minded dedication of people who accomplish so much— great industrialists, great athletes, great musicians? Try to emulate such people—their tenacity and their perseverance. Make a personal oath to succeed, and all the paperwork in the world won't stop you.

Epilogue

Procrastination and fear of the unknown are your deadliest enemies!

I know how easy it is to say, "Not now; maybe tomorrow," "My job takes all my time," "It's too risky," "I don't have the money," or "The market's not right." If you use any of these excuses to put off investing today, I promise you, years from now you'll sound like all the other procrastinators whom I call "Shoulda's"—"I shoulda bought this; I shoulda bought that."

When I was young, I got so tired of hearing my elders moan and groan over what they shoulda done that I vowed never to have that expression apply to me.

Procrastination is usually accompanied by fear of the unknown. We're all afraid of and put off doing things that are unfamiliar to us. But when the unknown becomes familiar, our fear disappears and we can take action. I can understand why an individual who has a safe, secure job will be reluctant—even fearful—of going out and investing hard-earned cash in what seems like a risky business. Taking risks and assuming new financial obligations could temporarily put a damper on such a person's lifestyle. But you know, that's exactly what the real estate investor must do! You cannot go from being a "timeclock puncheroo" to becoming financially independent without taking on some new responsibilities.

I always think in terms of success; you should too. I practically never ponder failure. But I know there are pessimists out there, and they do dwell on failure. For them, I offer this thought: Suppose you invest and your investment fails. How could that happen? Well, say that for the first time ever, the U.S. economy did not respond to the forces of market-oriented capitalism. In the unlikely event that that happens, what will you lose? Well, if you invested using the principles outlined in this book, very little.

On the other hand, when the opposite happens and our economy moves up to a new and even higher plateau of prosperity, you'll be grateful for the courage you showed and for the smart investment you made. The way I look at it, the consequences of the failure to invest are usually so much more severe than the consequences of an investment that failed. With the latter, you will have at least acquired some valuable knowledge—knowledge that could propel you to future triumphs.

You can't go back. Time lost is opportunity missed. When it comes to real estate investing, it's very unlikely that you'll be able to do tomorrow what you can do today.

Your first deal will be your most difficult. You'll be doing a lot of things for the first time, everything from selecting the right property to negotiating with your future buyer. After you wade your way through the first and second projects and make it to number three, you'll be devising your own methods of operation and you'll be laughing all the way to the bank.

I had a great time writing this book, sharing with you my experiences and tips. I know not every reader will blaze a trail toward becoming a real estate entrepreneur. But I commend those of you who will. You're the kind of spirited people our nation needs. Good luck!

Index

apartment buildings, 68-69, 189-210

appraisal, 95, 118, 125

appraised value, 23

appreciation, 6, 8, 9, 10, 74
  inflation and, 9-10

attorneys, 102, 136

auctions, 161-170, 191-192

bankruptcy, 168

brokers. *See* realtors.

building codes, 3

cash flow, 73, 87

closing costs, 116. *See also* escrow fees.

commission, realtor's, 25, 37, 43, 66, 67, 68, 69, 76, 136

condos, 171-178, 179-188

co-ops, 171-177, 178-179, 180-188

Consumer Credit Counseling Service (CCCS), 56

cosigner, 56-58

credit, 52-58, 86

credit cards, 58-60

credit report, 52, 53-54, 88, 89, 95

deed in lieu of foreclosure, 145-146

default notices, 43-44

distressed property, 1, 4, 7, 8, 11, 13, 15, 16, 31, 73, 129
  apartment buildings, 190-192
  condition of, 1-3
  environment and, 4, 31
  location and, 4, 31
  rehabilitation of, 2-3, 19, 21, 25, 26, 27, 34-36, 139, 204-205
  selecting, 17-39

sources of, 41-50

divorce filings, 44-45

down payment, 21, 26, 111-112, 116, 119, 122-123
  sources of, 51-64

earnest money, 37, 38, 158

escrow fees, 20, 25, 37, 71, 113, 143-144

Fair Credit Reporting Act, 89

Federal Home Loan Bank, 92

Federal Home Loan Mortgage Corporation (Freddie Mac), 92

Federal Housing Administration (FHA), 48, 85, 87, 90, 91, 92, 96, 98, 101, 111, 112-122, 133, 177

Federal National Mortgage Association (Fannie Mae), 91, 95, 103, 106

financing, 21-23, 26, 71-82, 85-109, 177-178. *See also* credit; down payment; mortgages.
  seller-assisted, 21-22, 23, 64-65, 74-82, 100-101

foreclosure, 22, 43, 44, 46, 47, 75, 82, 99-100, 113, 129-147, 149, 168. *See also* REOs.

Government National Mortgage Corporation (Ginnie Mae), 92

home improvement loan, 120

impound account, 116

inspections, 3, 24-25, 33

insurance, 95

interest rates, 105-108, 117, 123
investment, real estate as, 5-16

lenders, choosing, 93-94
leverage, 5-6, 81-82
liens, 33, 46, 49, 64, 75, 78, 79, 99, 139, 146. *See also* mortgages.
lines of credit, 60-62
loan application, 63-64, 86, 89-91, 94
  capacity and, 86-88
  character and, 88-89
  collateral and, 88

maintenance, deferred, 1-2, 3, 23, 24, 33, 192-193
mortgage brokers, 114, 116
mortgages, 22, 92, 95, 111. *See also* financing.
  assumable, 96-97, 116
  due-on-sale clauses, 96
  fees, 98-99
  FHA and, 112-122
  prepayment penalty, 98
  stable, 103-104
  subject-to clauses, 98
  VA and, 122-126
  variable-rate, 96, 98, 103, 104-108
  wrap-around, 99-102

National Association of Realtors, 43, 175
negative amortization, 105-106, 107
newspapers, 43, 130, 167, 192
"nothing down," 71-84
notices of default, 130, 134, 149

occupancy, 85-86, 116
offers, 37-38

permits for rehab, 3
personality traits of investor, 13-15
points, 98, 118
pricing of property, 7, 25-26, 27, 155, 197-203
private mortgage insurance (PMI), 21
probate, 44, 168
property profile, 34, 46
purchase of property, 19-26, 28, 30-39. *See also* auctions; financing; foreclosure; mortgages; REOs.
purchase transaction, 28-30

real estate agents. *See* realtors.
Real Estate Settlement Procedures Act (RESPA), 20, 108-109
realtors, 19, 27, 28, 42-43, 45, 48, 66-68, 69, 76, 87, 136, 175, 176
recordkeeping, 15, 211-220
  IRS and, 211-212
REOs, 41-42, 144, 149-159, 190
refinancing, 10-11, 74
rental income, 68, 87, 182-183, 195-196, 199, 203-204
Resolution Trust Corporation (RTC), 11, 46-48, 126-127
Rule of 72, 10

sale of property, 7, 8, 18, 19, 21, 25-30. *See also* auctions.
secondary mortgage market, 91-93
signature loans, 60-62
single-family houses, 17, 18, 19

taxes, 8, 11-12, 20, 75-76, 78, 186-187
Tax Reform Act of 1986, 186
tax sales, 45-46, 49-50, 168

title company, 34, 102
title insurance, 20
title report, 38, 39, 46
title search, 78
trading up, 208-210
trust deed, 21-22, 61, 64, 65, 66, 67, 69, 72, 75, 76, 77, 78, 79, 81-82, 96, 99-100, 102, 125-126, 133
trustee sales, 42, 43, 44, 144, 150-151, 152, 153

U.S. Department of Housing and Urban Development (HUD), 48-49, 90, 91, 112, 147

Veterans Administration (VA), 48, 85, 87-88, 90, 91, 92, 96, 98, 111, 112, 122-126, 133, 147

zero coupon bonds, 83-84

About the Author

Skip Lombardo is President of Lombardo Enterprises, a Southern California real estate development firm. He began his career in real estate with a modest investment in a Hollywood triplex and parlayed that investment into a multi-million dollar portfolio through property improvement, equity capitalization and exchanging techniques.

Inspired by a book on real estate investment, purchased in 1959, Mr. Lombardo has written this book, sharing his personal success story, with the hope of helping a new generation of aspiring real estate investors.

About the Publisher

PROBUS PUBLISHING COMPANY

Probus Publishing Company fills the informational needs of today's business professional by publishing authoritative, quality books on timely and relevant topics, including:

* Investing
* Futures/Options Trading
* Banking
* Finance
* Marketing and Sales
* Manufacturing and Project Management
* Personal Finance, Real Estate, Insurance and Estate Planning
* Entrepreneurship
* Management

Probus books are available at quantity discounts when purchased for business, educational or sales promotional use. For more information, please call the Director, Corporate/Institutional Sales at 1-800-PROBUS-1, or write:

Director, Corporate/Institutional Sales
Probus Publishing Company
1925 N. Clybourn Avenue
Chicago, Illinois 60614
FAX (312) 868-6250